EARLY YEARS
ACTIVITY CHEST

Assessment activities

British Library Cataloguing-in-Publication Data
A catalogue record for this book is available from the British Library.

ISBN 0 439 98486 6

ACKNOWLEDGEMENTS
The publishers gratefully acknowledge permission to reproduce the following copyright material:

Qualifications and Curriculum Authority for the use of extracts from the QCA/DfEE document *Curriculum Guidance for the Foundation Stage* © 2000, Qualifications and Curriculum Authority; **Qualifications and Curriculum Authority** for the use of extracts from the QCA/DfES document *Foundation Stage Profile* © 2002, Qualifications and Curriculum Authority.

Every effort has been made to trace copyright holders and the publishers apologise for any inadvertent omissions.

AUTHOR
Jean Evans

EDITOR
Jane Bishop

ASSISTANT EDITOR
Saveria Mezzana

SERIES DESIGNER
Lynne Joesbury

DESIGNER
Catherine Mason

ILLUSTRATIONS
Bethan Matthews/Sylvie Poggio Artists Agency

COVER PHOTOGRAPH
Martyn Chillmaid

Text © 2003 Jean Evans
© 2003 Scholastic Ltd
Designed using Adobe Pagemaker
Published by Scholastic Ltd, Villiers House,
Clarendon Avenue, Leamington Spa, Warwickshire CV32 5PR
Printed by Bell & Bain Ltd, Glasgow
Visit our website at www.scholastic.co.uk

2 3 4 5 6 7 8 9 0   3 4 5 6 7 8 9 0 1 2

CONTENTS

CONTENTS

Introduction

The *Early Years Activity Chest* series offers a wide range of interactive activities for children aged three to five years. The aim of this book is to suggest how early years practitioners can observe children as they take part in everyday activities, and use these observations for assessing and recording their progress across all six Areas of Learning. Emphasis is made on the importance of effective questioning and the use of appropriate language in order to evaluate children's knowledge and understanding at the time of assessment.

This book will be particularly useful for practitioners who are completing the *Foundation Stage Profile Booklet* (QCA), as suggestions are given for gathering evidence linked to the points within the assessment scales in this document for each activity. The importance of observing the child in familiar situations, for example, taking part in daily routines and regular curriculum activities, rather than setting up 'test' activities, is emphasised. With this in mind, activities have been chosen that are related to the everyday experiences of most early years settings, using readily obtainable resources.

The *Foundation Stage Profile Handbook* (QCA) provides the framework for this book, and the activities and assessment suggestions support the document. However, this book also provides an appropriate balance of activities and assessment suggestions for those early years practitioners who are not involved in the Foundation Stage, and the activities within it are equally applicable to the early years documents on pre-school education published in Scotland, Wales and Northern Ireland.

For more information and to download the *Foundation Stage Profile Handbook* and *Booklet*, visit the QCA website at www.qca.org.uk

The importance of assessment

One of the principles for early years education in the *Curriculum Guidance for the Foundation Stage* (QCA) states that 'Practitioners must be able to observe and respond appropriately to children in order to help them to make progress'.

Early years practitioners are already assessing children informally in many different ways as they work with them, for example, observing their day to day progress, sharing their experiences, discovering their interests and finding out about their personal likes and dislikes. This informal assessment is an ongoing process. However, a formal system is needed to ensure that all aspects of a child's development are monitored carefully.

Assessing children's attainment and progress is an essential part of the planning cycle, providing staff with the information that they need to build successfully on what a child already knows and is interested in, and to identify any gaps in their knowledge. They can then plan and organise new learning activities and experiences so that the

children can move confidently to the next stage of their development. As they evaluate the success of these planned learning opportunities, staff can adjust future plans accordingly, for example, deciding whether individual children will need support, or including ways of extending activities for those who are more able. The activity pages in this book make suggestions for differentiation to meet individual needs through 'Support' and 'Extension' sections.

Assessment should be an ongoing process, from the initial assessment on entry to a setting to the final assessment before moving on to the next stage of education. This will provide a full picture of a child's developmental progress over a longer term and determine a child's achievements at a given point in time.

The importance of observation

Observation is an essential part of planning and assessment. It is a means of discovering exactly what a child can do and say, and avoids the possibility of assumptions based on what the child is expected to be doing. Watching and listening as children work and play is of greater benefit than concentrating on analysing the end product of their actions. Observations should be a manageable part of the routine of the setting and need to involve all members of staff. When considering how to organise effective observation, ensure that individual staff members are given time, free from other duties, to focus on a particular child or small group, and plan time for sharing the results of observations so that the children's progress can be evaluated. While observing, try not to distract the child, by standing well back from the action. If necessary, ask appropriate questions and discuss any problems that the child encounters during the activity in order to clarify the adult interpretation of a child's understanding. Jot down spontaneous observations as they happen, perhaps on a 'Post-it' note, so that they can be added to a child's records later. Complete fuller observations in a diary or notebook. Listen carefully to the language that the child uses, and make note of this.

Consider observing an individual child playing alone, working with an adult or sharing an activity with a group of friends. Make observations in different play areas, both indoors and outdoors. Notice in particular a child's social interactions, language development and physical skills.

Keeping records

Keeping records for individual children in your setting enables personal achievements at a given moment to be celebrated, demonstrated and reinforced. Sharing records with parents and carers helps them to be more aware of their children's progress and to share in their achievements. Referring to records helps staff to plan for a child to move on to the next stage of their development with confidence. Any significant skills or difficulties will be identified so that staff can work with parents, carers and other professionals to plan appropriate experiences to meet the needs of those who require further challenge and those who need additional support.

Record-keeping systems vary considerably and it is important that the chosen system suit the staff,

children, parents and carers within a setting. Such a system may include, for example, a child's personal details; their medical or dietary requirements; an initial record of their achievements on entry; observations of their activities, behaviour and language; ongoing records of achievement, and samples of work and photographs.

Information from these records can be transferred to the Foundation Stage Profile during the final term before entering Key Stage 1 of the National Curriculum to help to give a full picture of a child's overall developmental progress and achievement.

The involvement of parents and carers

It is important to involve parents and carers in the assessment process from when a child first enters a setting. They know a great deal about many aspects of their child's development and often exchange this information informally with staff during daily discussions at the beginning and end of a session. More formal contributions can also be encouraged, for example, by inviting parents and carers to complete an 'All about me' booklet about their child, or to take part in discussions at review meetings.

More effective contributions can be encouraged by supplying information to increase parents and carers' understanding of how a child learns and the significant developmental milestones. They should be well informed about the curriculum, for example, through attractive displays and brochures in their home languages.

The involvement of the child

Children should be involved in the assessment process from the start, for example, by choosing particular pieces of work to include in a folder, 'writing' comments in their own diaries, or drawing 'happy' or 'sad' faces to indicate their preferences. They should be encouraged to discuss their feelings, as well as their likes and dislikes, with confidence so that they realise that their opinions and contributions are respected and valued.

The involvement of other contributors

All adults working with a particular child within the setting should contribute to the assessment of that child's progress, including, for example, additional language or special needs support assistants. Support staff from outside agencies, such as speech therapists, should also be consulted in their particular area of expertise. It may also be relevant to invite contributions from other adults involved with the child, such as a childminder or member of staff from an after-school club.

The *Foundation Stage Profile*

This document is designed to be used during each child's final year of the Foundation Stage to record their progress towards the Early Learning Goals. It can be completed either as an ongoing record of a child's achievement throughout the Reception year, or during the summer term of that year to summarise a child's development at that point. If other record-keeping systems are used in the setting, information from these can be transferred on to the Profile during the summer term.

The Profile includes all six Areas of Learning in order to provide a full picture of a child's development at the end of the Foundation Stage. The six Areas of Learning are divided into 13 assessment scales, and each of these has nine points against which the children are assessed.

The first three points describe a child who is still progressing towards the achievements described in the Early Learning Goals, and these are mainly based on the Stepping Stones. The next five points are drawn from the Early Learning Goals and are presented in approximate order of difficulty, but are not necessarily hierarchical. Point 9 on each scale describes a child who has achieved all the preceding eight points on that scale and is working consistently beyond the level of the Early Learning Goals and within the early levels of the National Curriculum.

The points on the assessment scales have been devised with the aim of breaking down the Early Learning Goals so that practitioners can make a straightforward 'yes' or 'no' judgement of a child's progress for each point. Making such a judgement will usually be based on a practitioner's existing knowledge, and on information taken from the records of the child. However, sometimes there will be a need for additional information before a judgement can be made. It may be necessary to carry out further observations, for example, of a child's behaviour in different contexts. It is important that these contexts should be part of your everyday provision rather than set up specifically for the purpose of assessment. The *Foundation Stage Profile* includes case studies to demonstrate how assessment observations can be integrated into your daily routines and activities.

The activities in this book have been chosen because they are common to most early years settings, either as popular topic-based curriculum activities or as regular play experiences, for example, in sand and water areas. They will provide added opportunities for assessment observations.

Children with special educational needs

'The Foundation Stage Profile has been developed to be inclusive, so that as many children as possible can be assessed against the scales it contains'. (*Foundation Stage Profile Handbook*). This has been achieved by providing examples relating to children with different individual needs, providing guidance on assessment for such children and cross-referencing items in the Profile scales to 'P scales'. Further advice on assessment of children with special educational needs can be found in the *Foundation Stage Profile Handbook* (see page 5).

English as an additional language

Assessments in the *Foundation Stage Profile* address three aspects of the achievements of children for whom English is an additional language: development in their home language, development across the curriculum assessed through the home language, and the development of English. The Profile includes an 'English as an additional language' section so that children's development in their home languages can be noted. This will help practitioners to provide appropriate experiences as the child begins to move into English, and also help to identify any language delay or disorder, or other special needs. With appropriate bilingual support, children can be assessed in all the scales in all Areas of Learning, apart from Communication, language and literacy, where Points 4 to 9 must be assessed in English. The comments boxes on each scale of the Profile can also be used to record achievements made through the medium of English. If home-language support is not available and it is not possible to access the child's full understanding as a result, this can be noted in the boxes. Further information can be found in the *Foundation Stage Profile Handbook* (see page 5).

How to use this book

There are six activity chapters in this book, and each covers one of the six Areas of the Early Learning Goals (QCA). The chapters are based on the assessment scales in the *Foundation Stage Profile* and, as such, vary in length.

■ Chapter 1: 'Personal, social and emotional development'
The 16 activity pages cover the nine points for three assessment scales: Dispositions and attitudes (six activities), Social development (five) and Emotional development (five).

■ Chapter 2: 'Communication, language and literacy'
The 20 activity pages cover the nine points for four assessment scales: Language for communication and thinking (five activities), Linking sounds and letters (five), Reading (five) and Writing (five).

■ Chapter 3: 'Mathematical development'
The 16 pages cover the nine points for three assessment scales: Numbers as labels and for counting (five activities), Calculating (five) and Shape, space and measures (six).

■ Chapter 4: 'Knowledge and understanding of the world'
The six pages cover the nine points for one assessment scale.

■ Chapter 5: 'Physical development'
The six pages cover the nine points for one assessment scale.

■ Chapter 6: 'Creative development'
The six pages cover the nine points for one assessment scale.

Within each assessment scale, all of the nine points are used as a focus for an activity at least once. Frequently, more than one point is visited in a single activity and, occasionally, different aspects of a single point are focused upon in separate activities.

The activity pages

Each activity page is organised in the same way. A main learning objective is given, based on one of the Early Learning Goals. Occasionally, where appropriate, more than one learning objective is given. Links are made with one of the Foundation Stage Profile assessment scales and the relevant points along that scale. In order to support these links, suggestions that practitioners may like to consider for observation are included under the heading 'Assessment', these being linked back to the numbered Foundation Stage Profile assessment scales. These suggestions are intended as a guide as to what an individual child could be achieving as they take part in the activity.

Recommendations are given for group size and timing in each activity, although these are only guidelines. Practitioners should be flexible according to the needs of individual children and of the group as a whole.

A list of appropriate resources is included, under the heading 'What you need', and guidance about preparation for the activity is given as a separate paragraph where necessary. The simple step-by-step 'What to do' guidance will be particularly useful for practitioners with less practical experience. Those with greater experience will already be familiar with many of the activities and prefer to use a different method of approach that suits their setting and the accommodation and resources available. 'Support' and 'Extension' sections suggest practical ways of adapting the idea to meet the needs of younger or less able children, and extending it to challenge those who are older or more able. These suggestions will enable practitioners to organise the activity to suit individuals so that they can focus their observations on a particular point along the assessment scale.

'Home links' provides ways of involving parents and carers in the activity, and extending it by further activities at home. This section also helps to establish links between home and the setting, for example, as parents and carers provide additional resources for an activity or share a particular skill with the staff or children.

CHAPTER 1

Offer a range of opportunities to assess the children's dispositions and attitudes, social development and emotional development as they explore and play together.

Personal, social and emotional development

Dispositions and attitudes

• • • • • •

1 Shows an interest in classroom activities through observation or participation.

• • • • • •

6 Continues to be interested, motivated and excited to learn.

GROUP SIZE
Four children.

TIMING
20 minutes.

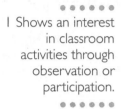

ASSESSMENT
Observe whether the child shows curiosity during the activity. Does he or she demonstrate motivation by watching attentively and listening to what is said? Note how readily the child joins in, with adult support if necessary. Does he or she show excitement when taking part, and anticipate what will happen next?

HOME LINKS
Send home instructions so that the children and their carers can create their own jelly ponds.

POND HIDE-AND-SEEK

Learning objective
To continue to be interested, excited and motivated to learn.

What you need
A packet of green jelly; blue food colouring; tablespoon; measuring jug; kettle; shallow, transparent plastic bowl; jelly worms and fish; sweet 'shoelaces'; four dessertspoons and serving bowls.

What to do
Talk about pond creatures and suggest that the children make an edible pond. Show them the tablet of jelly and observe how it is divided into cubes. Give them a strip of four cubes each. Ask them to count them, break the strip into single cubes and put each cube into the jug.

Boil the kettle at a safe distance from the children. Add boiling water to the half-pint mark in the jug and stir until the jelly has dissolved. Add cold water slowly to the pint mark, then take the jelly over to the children and invite them to take turns to stir the dissolved solution.

Pour the jelly into the shallow bowl and observe the colour. Add one drop of blue food colouring and watch as it spreads through the green liquid.

Show the children the jelly worms and fish and ask them to choose two things to put into the pond. Add sweet 'shoelaces' to represent pond weed and leave the jelly to set. Supply each child with a dessertspoon and a small bowl and invite them to take turns to help themselves to the jelly. Have fun eating the 'catch' and the 'pond water'.

Support
With younger children, make individual ponds by asking them to pour the dissolved jelly into clear plastic cups, then inviting them to drop in their pond creatures.

Extension
Talk to older children about the differences between solids and liquids, and encourage them to observe the various changes as the jelly dissolves.

**FOUNDATION
STAGE PROFILE
LINKS**

Dispositions and
attitudes

• • • • • •

2 Dresses,
undresses and
manages own
personal hygiene
with adult support.

• • • • • •

4 Dresses and
undresses
independently and
manages own
personal hygiene.

GROUP SIZE
Four children.

TIMING
20 minutes.

ASSESSMENT
Observe the children as they dress and
undress. Are they fully independent? Do
they come to an adult for help with some
parts of the task, but manage others unaided? Note
any skills that require further practice, such as fastening
buttons or pulling up zips on shorts, and support the
children with these during future activities.

HOME LINKS

Invite parents and
carers to donate
beach clothes in
larger sizes. Explain
the learning
objective of the
activity and suggest
that they develop
their children's
dressing skills at
home by gradually
giving less assistance
and introducing
more complex
fastenings.

DOWN BY THE SEA

Learning objective
To dress and undress independently.

What you need
A large piece of blue fabric; large piece of yellow fabric; shells; buckets;
spades; toy boats; four rucksacks; four sets of beach wear in a large size to
include T-shirts, shorts, sun-hats and sandals; four beach towels.

Preparation
Create a beach by arranging yellow and blue fabric on the floor. Add
shells, buckets and spades and toy boats on the 'sand'.

What to do
Explain to the children that they are going for an imaginary seaside visit.
Invite each child to pack a rucksack with what they need, including a
beach towel, sun-hat, pair of shorts, T-shirt and sandals. Make a pretend
journey around the room to the beach that you have created.

Suggest that the children spread out their beach towels and put on the
clothes that they have brought. Explain that they must put these over
their own clothes, as it is only 'pretend', but that they can take off their
shoes and socks and put on the sandals.

Play freely at the beach, building sand-castles and paddling in the sea.
When it is time to go home, suggest that the children remove their beach
wear and pack the clothes and towels back in the rucksacks.

Support
Show younger children how to cope with any difficult fastenings, such as
buckles. Encourage them to manage for themselves, but support them if
they become frustrated.

Introduce more complex role-play for older children, such as a visit to
a dance class on a winter's day, to encourage them to attempt a variety
of fastenings.

Extension
Introduce more complex role-play for older children, such as a visit to
a dance class on a winter's day to encourage them to attempt a variety
of fastenings.

FOUNDATION STAGE PROFILE LINKS

Dispositions and attitudes

• • • • • •

3 Displays high levels of involvement in self-chosen activities.

• • • • • •

9 Sustains involvement and perseveres, particularly when trying to solve a problem or reach a satisfactory conclusion.

GROUP SIZE
Four children.

TIMING
20 minutes.

ASSESSMENT
Do the children demonstrate a high level of involvement in this chosen activity? (3)

Does each child show reluctance to leave the activity until the task is completed satisfactorily, and a readiness to return to the activity if there is an interruption? (9)

HOME LINKS
Explain the learning objective to parents and carers and suggest that they present their children with simple problems when playing with construction equipment at home, for example, creating enclosures for toy farm animals.

BUILDING BRIDGES

Learning objective
To continue to be interested, excited and motivated to learn.

What you need
A water tray; small stones; blue food colouring; four small-world characters; plastic construction equipment; wood offcuts; recycled plastic containers.

Preparation
Half-fill a water tray with water and add a few drops of blue food colouring. Arrange the small stones in two piles at each end to represent islands. Make sure that some of the stones are above the surface of the water. Stand the four small-world characters on one of the islands. Arrange the construction equipment, wood offcuts and plastic containers on a table alongside.

What to do
Explain the activities that are on offer at the start of the session, including the opportunity to build boats and bridges in the water tray. Encourage the children to make their own choices.

When four children have gathered at the water tray, explain that the small-world characters are stuck on the island. They need to cross to the other island but the water is too deep.

Invite each child to choose a small-world character and to find a way for that character to travel between the islands using the resources on the table. Encourage the children to consider different options using the resources, such as constructing bridges or making ferryboats.

Support
Simply add plastic boats or shallow trays to the water so that younger children can transport characters easily between the islands.

Extension
Challenge older children by suggesting that they create life jackets, for example, using corks or bubble wrap, so that the characters will be safe if they fall into the sea during the crossing.

GROUP SIZE
Four children.

TIMING
Ten minutes.

ASSESSMENT
Is the child able to make the necessary links between the resources provided and the play areas? When in the chosen play area, is the child able to select confidently from the range of equipment provided and move to another activity independently?

IT'S YOUR CHOICE

Learning objective
To select and use activities and resources independently.

What you need
Items associated with different play areas, such as a paintbrush, sand scoop, plastic brick and book; tray; name cards; wall hanging to store name cards; a plastic container for each play area; card; felt-tipped pen; sticky tape.

Preparation
Create a number card for each play area to indicate how many children can play in that area, and tape it to a container. Leave an appropriately numbered container in each play area. Find suitable items to represent each play area.

What to do
Arrange the play resources on the tray, then put the tray on the floor with the wall hanging near by. Invite the children to sit around the tray and explain that you would like them to find something on it that is linked to their favourite play area.

Ask them to take turns to pick up their chosen object and to talk about what they might do with it before replacing it on the tray. Once all the children have talked about an object, ask each child to take their name card from the wall hanging, go to their chosen area and deposit the name card in the container before playing.

Once the required number of children have deposited name cards in the container for a particular area, any extra children must choose another area until there is a free space.

Support
Put more items on the tray for younger children and ask them to choose something and take it straight to the appropriate play area, rather than wait for the others and choose name cards.

Extension
Encourage older children to choose two or three activities for the session from a selection of picture cards, then ask each child to put the picture cards alongside their name card on the wall hanging before going to their first chosen play area.

HOME LINKS
Encourage parents and carers to give their children choices, for example, at mealtimes or when shopping, to encourage independence.

FOUNDATION STAGE PROFILE LINKS

Dispositions and attitudes

• • • • • •

7 Is confident to try new activities, initiate ideas and speak in a familiar group.

GROUP SIZE

Six children.

TIMING

20 minutes.

A FRUITY SELECTION

Learning objective
To be confident to try new activities, initiate ideas and speak in a familiar group.

What you need
A plastic tray; six different kinds of fruit, two samples of each; drawstring bag.

Preparation
Ensure that the samples of each type of fruit match closely in size, shape and colour. Put one sample of each fruit into the drawstring bag and the other on to the tray.

What to do
Invite the children to sit around a tray of six different pieces of fruit and ask them if they can name them. Pass around the 'feely bag' containing matching samples and invite the children to guess what is inside. Can they make suggestions about how they could discover more about the contents without tipping them out?

Ask each child to take turns to put a hand in the bag and choose a piece of fruit to describe. Encourage the child to talk about the size, shape and texture.

Invite the listening children to guess which fruit is being described, then ask the child to lift it out and match it to a piece of fruit on the tray. Were the children's guesses correct?

When all the children have had a turn, enjoy tasting the fruit together.

ASSESSMENT

Does the child enter into the activity with confidence and speak clearly in front of the others? Does he or she make suggestions or initiate ideas in response to adult questions?

HOME LINKS

Explain the activity to parents and carers and suggest that they introduce new experiences to their children, such as tasting unusual fruit. Emphasise the importance of encouraging children to discuss what they like or dislike about their experiences.

Support
Develop younger children's confidence by using familiar fruit with contrasting appearances, such as an apple and a banana. Ask them to point to the matching fruit on the tray if they have difficulty in describing it. Support them by modelling vocabulary and talking about their choices.

Extension
Encourage older children to take initiative by inviting them to think of similar activities involving guessing things without seeing them, for example, using blindfolds or feeling under a cloth.

FOUNDATION STAGE PROFILE LINKS
Dispositions and attitudes

● ● ● ● ● ●

8 Maintains attention and concentrates.

GROUP SIZE
Four children.

TIMING
Ten to 15 minutes.

ASSESSMENT
Does the child sit quietly and listen attentively to instructions and then concentrate on the given task? Does he or she become highly absorbed in the activity, oblivious of distractions?

HOME LINKS
Encourage parents and carers to increase their children's ability to concentrate and sit quietly, for example, by playing table-top games with them or reading stories.

LOOK, NO HANDS!

Learning objective
To maintain attention, concentrate, and sit quietly when appropriate.

What you need
A selection of utensils for lifting small objects, such as spoons, tweezers, tongs, scoops and salad servers; four different types of small objects, such as marbles, conkers, beads and seeds; four plastic plates; four small bowls.

Preparation
Place the small objects on separate plates and arrange the plates in a row on the carpet, with a good space between them. Make a row of bowls opposite the plates and leave the utensils in between.

What to do
Invite the children to sit quietly on the carpet and to listen to what you have planned. Show them the resources and explain that you want to move the things on the plates to the bowls opposite. Ask the children if they would like to do this for you. Emphasise that they must try not to touch the objects with their hands but should use the utensils instead.

Invite each child to choose a different plate of objects to transfer to the bowl opposite. Allow a few minutes for the children to try out the utensils and start moving the objects before stopping the activity and asking them how they are managing. Have they found the best utensil to lift their chosen object? Suggest that they change places with another child and try moving a different object this time. Did they use the same utensil, or was another more suitable?

Support
Avoid frustration by simplifying the task for younger children with larger utensils, such as a plastic ladle, and objects that will not roll away from them, such as wooden cubes. Praise them for their actions and support them if necessary.

Extension
Challenge older children by presenting them with tiny items, such as grains of rice, and small utensils such as tweezers. Show that you value their ability to concentrate and persevere, but support them if the task is too difficult, before they become frustrated.

ASSESSMENT
Does the child work comfortably alongside others engaged in the same activity and happily share the same materials and resources?

JUST ADD WATER

Learning objective
To form good relationships with adults and peers.

What you need
Four shallow trays; large jug; large plastic spoon; cornflour; water; four aprons; bowl of water; paper towels.

Preparation
Mix some cornflour with a small amount of water in a jug and gradually add more water. Experiment with the amount of cornflour needed to form a thick creamy consistency.

What to do
Talk to the children about the choices of activity at the start of the session and explain to them how you are going to make a 'gooey' mixture that is fun to play with.

Set out the four trays at a table and cover the bottom of each tray with a layer of the cornflour mixture that you have made. Encourage the children who choose to play at the table to put on an apron and to roll up their sleeves before starting experimenting with the mixture. Arrange washing facilities near by if the cloakroom is not easily accessible, so that the children can wash their hands when they have finished.

Let the children play freely alongside each other, exploring how the mixture looks, feels and reacts when they spread fingers across it or try to lift it in the air. Share their enjoyment and ask questions about their actions and observations. Draw their attention to the other children by commenting on their actions. Show that you value the actions of all the children, so that they begin to feel part of the group even when playing at their own tray.

Support
Younger children may feel reluctant to share this new experience at first. Encourage them to watch as you put your hands into the mixture and swirl it around. Demonstrate that you are happy for them to join in when they feel ready.

Extension
Invite older children to help to make the mixture and to pour it into their trays. Encourage them to share their observations with those around them while still having their own personal space.

FOUNDATION STAGE PROFILE LINKS
Social development

● ● ● ● ● ●

2 Builds relationships through gesture and talk.

● ● ● ● ● ●

5 Forms good relationships with adults and peers.

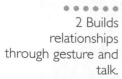

GROUP SIZE
Four children.

TIMING
Ten minutes each to write the invitation and the letter.

ASSESSMENT
Is the child able to communicate through facial expressions and gestures, for example, smiling and waving to a visitor, or passing a piece of equipment to another child? (2)

Is the child friendly and welcoming towards others, showing courtesy and speaking politely? (5)

HOME LINKS
Suggest that parents and carers invite their children to help to write their own party invitations and 'thank you' letters.

WELCOME TO OUR GROUP!

Learning objective
To form good relationships with adults and peers.

What you need
A sheet of A4 card; A4 envelope; felt-tipped pens; adult-size chair; cushion; length of bright fabric; biscuits; fruit juice; tray; plastic plate and cup; doily.

Preparation
Prepare some biscuits with a group of children the day before the visitor arrives.

What to do
Discuss the possibility of inviting someone special to talk to the children about their topic. Encourage the children to make suggestions and decide who is to be the invited guest, for example, a fire officer, florist, post person or farmer.

Invite the children to help to write an invitation to the visitor. Discuss the information that the visitor will need, such as the venue, date and time, and scribe this for the children on a sheet of card. Ask them to help to decorate the invitation with their own drawings and patterns, and involve them in posting it.

Talk about ways of making the visitor feel welcome on the day of the visit. Prepare a special seat, for example, by adding a cushion and draping it with fabric. Set out a tray with a plate of the home-made biscuits displayed on a doily alongside a drink of fruit juice.

Discuss with the children how they might make the visitor feel welcome, for example, by inviting him or her to join their play and explaining what they are doing.

Follow up the visit with a 'thank you' letter from the whole group.

Support
Younger children may feel shy in the company of a stranger. Emphasise that the visitor is a friend and arrange for familiar members of staff to sit beside any children who feel anxious.

Extension
Encourage older children to greet the visitor, show him or her around the setting and serve the refreshments.

GIANT DICE

Learning objective
To work as part of a group or class, taking turns and sharing fairly.

What you need
Cube-shaped box; yellow paint; black paper; tape; beanbags; hoops; PVA glue; selection of dice of different sizes from children's games.

Preparation
Seal the lid of the box with tape. Paint the whole box yellow and allow the paint to dry. Cut out 21 black paper circles and glue them to the sides of the box in the correct positions to form a large dice. Cover the dice with PVA glue to protect the surface, and allow this to dry.

What to do
Show the children the selection of dice and talk about their experiences of dice games. Pass around the large dice and suggest that the children use it to invent their own games. Move to a clear space indoors or outdoors, taking the dice and some beanbags and hoops.

Try out the children's ideas and your suggestions. For example, take turns to throw the dice, pick up the number of beanbags indicated by the dots, drop them in a hoop and then count them after a given number of throws.

Stop the games and talk about the simple rules involved, emphasising the words 'take turns' and 'share'. What would happen if the children did not take turns and share the equipment?

Support
Make a dice with two sets of up to three spots for younger children. Work as a group towards the same goal, for example, filling the hoop with beanbags, rather than competing against one another.

Extension
Challenge older children by encouraging them to play team games in small groups. For example, they could build towers with wooden or plastic blocks, using the number of blocks corresponding to the number of dots on the dice, in a given time, to see which team has the highest tower when time is up.

Social development

• • • • • •

6 Understands that
there need to be
agreed values and
codes of behaviour
for groups of
people, including
adults and children,
to work together
harmoniously.

• • • • • •

9 Takes into account
the ideas of others.

GROUP SIZE
Four children.

TIMING
20 minutes.

ASSESSMENT

Does the child follow the rules created
for using apparatus, and does he or she
understand the consequences of not
adhering to them? (6)

Is the child able to work collaboratively with others
and take into account their ideas, for example, when
creating the list of safety rules? (9)

HOME LINKS
Encourage parents
and carers to devise
simple 'house rules',
such as helping to
prepare meals and
tidy up.

APPARATUS CODE

Learning objective
To understand that there needs to be agreed values and codes of behaviour
for groups of people, including adults and children, to work together
harmoniously.

What you need
A selection of large apparatus such as a climbing frame, slide, barrel and
tunnel; safety mats; small apparatus such as balls, beanbags and hoops;
large sheets of card; black felt-tipped pen; easel.

Preparation
Set out the large apparatus to include examples of safety hazards, for
example, placing a barrel at the bottom of a slide. Distribute the small
apparatus on and around the large equipment.

What to do
Explain to the children that the apparatus has already been set out, but
that you want them to help you to check that it is safe.

Stand at the side of the area and discuss any obvious hazards created by
the large apparatus. Invite the children to watch while you move the
apparatus into a safe position.

Talk about the small apparatus. Should the children play with balls and
beanbags near to large apparatus? Ask them to pick up the small items
and put them back into storage containers.

Invite the children to sit in front of the easel and explain
that you want to be sure that they use the apparatus safely
and fairly. Scribe for them as they contribute their own
ideas about how this can be achieved.

Work collaboratively to decide on a set of simple rules.
Write the rules on a fresh sheet of card and display it in
the appropriate area.

Support
Remind younger children about appropriate behaviour
before they use apparatus, and praise them for
remembering rules such as holding safety rails.

Extension
Involve older children in creating rules for using equipment outdoors.

FOUNDATION STAGE PROFILE LINKS

Social development

• • • • • •

7 Understands that people have different needs, views, cultures and beliefs that need to be treated with respect.

• • • • • •

8 Understands that s/he can expect others to treat her or his needs, views, cultures and beliefs with respect.

GROUP SIZE

Up to eight children.

TIMING

Ten to 15 minutes.

ASSESSMENT

Does the child enjoy sharing his or her own cultural traditions and religious beliefs, and show that he or she values and respects cultural and religious differences? (7)

Is the child demonstrating a positive self-image, showing that he or she is comfortable with himself or herself? (8)

HOME LINKS

Invite parents and carers to talk about their own experiences of festivals of light.

FESTIVALS OF LIGHT

Learning objective

To understand that people have different needs, views, cultures and beliefs that need to be treated with respect.

What you need

Clay; tea lights; decorative candles; tall advent candles; hanukiah; pictures of Divali, Hanukkah and Christmas; large tray; ribbon.

Preparation

Arrange a display of candles that includes decorative candles, advent candles, a hanukiah and diva lamps made from clay. Back the display with pictures of various festivals of light.

What to do

Talk to the children about the candle display and their experiences of candles, for example, on a birthday cake or in their place of worship. Explain to the children that light is used as a symbol in many different religious festivals. Let them handle the candles and the diva lamps, and point out a hanukiah and advent candles on the pictures if these are not easily obtained.

Ask each child in turn to choose a candle from the display and put it on the tray in the middle of the carpet. Form a large circle with ribbon around the tray and ask the children to sit outside it. Explain that they must stay behind this ribbon because candles are dangerous when they are lit.

Darken the room as much as possible and light the candles. Tell the story of Divali and the significance of the lighted lamps. Talk about the significance of the nine candles on a hanukiah during the festival of Hanukkah. Discuss how advent candles are lit leading up to Christmas Day.

Support

Tell just one story to younger children and light one candle in the centre of the circle.

Extension

Encourage older children to describe their feelings as they watch the candles in the darkened room.

HERE I AM!

Learning objective
To have a developing awareness of their own needs, views and feelings and be sensitive to the needs, views and feelings of others.

What you need
A set of the children's name cards; small-world farm animals (one for each child in the whole group); farm layout; storage containers for name cards and animals.

What to do
Talk to the children about their arrival routines. Encourage them to talk about their feelings when they leave their parents or carers. What do they do on arrival? Explain the significance of finding name cards on a table and putting them in a container so that staff know who is present at each session.

Show the children the container of farm animals and explain that the animals want to play. Suggest that the children each choose an animal as they arrive and put it somewhere on the farm layout. Perhaps they will choose a sheep and put it alongside another sheep as a friend, or they may decide to put a duck on the pond or a horse in the field.

Display a notice in the entrance so that parents and carers can help their children to take part in the 'arrival' activity.

The following day, once most of the children have taken part in the activity, take a small group over to the farm layout. Discuss where the children have put the animals. Will the number of children match the number of animals and name cards? Count to check.

Vary the arrival activity regularly, for example, using a doll's house, zoo layout or dinosaur landscape.

Support
Encourage younger children to leave their main carer happily by joining them as they take part in the activity and accompanying them to the next activity of their choice.

Extension
Encourage older children to look out for younger children who might be feeling insecure on arrival and to invite them to join their play.

FOUNDATION STAGE PROFILE LINKS

Emotional development

• • • • • •

2 Communicates freely about home and community.

• • • • • •

6 Has a developing respect for own culture and beliefs and those of other people.

GROUP SIZE

Up to 12 children.

TIMING

20 minutes.

ASSESSMENT

Does the child talk freely about events at home and bring things to show to the rest of the group? (2)

Does the child understand that certain events and objects are important to their own culture and beliefs or to those of other people? (6)

A GROUP WEDDING

Learning objective

To have a developing respect for their own cultures and beliefs and those of other people.

What you need

Photographs and artefacts related to weddings that the children have attended, such as an invitation, confetti and order of service; bridal party costumes or party clothes; plastic flowers; snack food.

Preparation

Research into the wedding traditions of various cultures beforehand to ensure accuracy. Put up a notice requesting wedding outfits, photographs of weddings and artefacts to display. Collect together old party and wedding clothes donated by parents and carers to cut down and create bridal outfits for the children.

What to do

Talk to the children about their experiences of weddings in their culture and look at the photographs and artefacts that they have brought in.

Set up a role-play wedding, for example, a Christian or Muslim ceremony, and invite someone from a local place of worship to officiate. Choose children to play the bridal party and ask the other children to act as guests.

Transform a clear floor area into the place of worship, for example, by arranging chairs in rows to represent a church. After the service, invite the children to sit at tables and enjoy the reception of appropriate foods, such as an iced cake for a Christian wedding.

Follow up the experience by comparing wedding traditions that the children are familiar with, with those of other cultures.

Support

Younger children will enjoy simply dressing up in the clothes and playing 'Weddings' rather than acting out a ceremony.

Extension

Take older children to visit a place of worship, such as a mosque, synagogue or church, and arrange for them to be taken on a tour, where significant features are pointed out to them.

HOME LINKS

Invite parents and carers from different cultures, or with different beliefs, to share their wedding-ceremony traditions with the children.

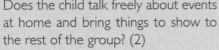

FOUNDATION STAGE PROFILE LINKS

Emotional development

● ● ● ● ● ●

3 Expresses needs and feelings in appropriate ways.

● ● ● ● ● ●

5 Has a developing awareness of own needs, views and feelings and is sensitive to the needs, views and feelings of others.

GROUP SIZE

Four children.

TIMING
15 minutes.

ASSESSMENT
Is the child able to express a preference with confidence? (3)

Can the child give reasons for likes and dislikes? Is he or she able to listen to the preferences of others and appreciate that not everyone shares the same taste? (5)

HOME LINKS

Explain to parents and carers the importance of giving choices to their children and of encouraging them to express their preferences.

THE BAKER'S SHOP

Learning objective
To have a developing awareness of their own needs, views and feelings and be sensitive to the needs, views and feelings of others.

What you need
Examples of different kinds of breads, for example, granary, pitta, chapatti, ciabatta, cottage loaf and baguette; soft spread; small and large plates; napkins.

Preparation
Ask for permission from parents and carers to taste foods and check for any food allergies and dietary requirements. Purchase a wide selection of breads with differing colour, texture and taste, and find out their country of origin.

What to do
Display the breads on plates in the centre of a table and invite the children to wash their hands and come to the table. Explain to them that you have been shopping to find types of breads. Do they recognise any of the breads on the plates? Can they name them?

Pass around the whole loaves first and talk about their colour, shape, smell and size. Does the smell of the bread make them feel hungry? What do the children do when they feel hungry?

Cut one of the loaves into bite-size pieces and invite the children to taste them. If they find the bread dry, suggest that they add some soft spread. Talk about the colour of the bread and the texture. Is it smooth or rough? Did they enjoy tasting the bread?

Continue to try the different breads and to make comparisons between them.

Emphasise to the children that not everyone shares the same tastes and that they should respect differences.

Support
Limit younger children to two contrasting breads, for example, a white soft roll and a brown wholemeal loaf, and invite them to express their preferences.

Extension
Help older children to find out more about the country of origin of the breads. Make a graph of preferences.

FOUNDATION STAGE PROFILE LINKS
Emotional development

• • • • • •

7 Considers the consequences of words and actions for self and others.

• • • • • •

8 Understands what is right, what is wrong, and why.

GROUP SIZE
Four children.

TIMING
Ten minutes.

ASSESSMENT
Is the child aware of the consequences of his or her words or actions on others, and is this awareness apparent in how the child behaves towards others, for example, when inviting another child to join in or share a piece of equipment? (7)

Does the child understand the difference between right and wrong and is this demonstrated in his or her behaviour, such as when following simple rules for handling sand and sharing equipment fairly? (8)

HOME LINKS
Encourage parents and carers to talk to their children about their actions and to help them to realise the consequences of inappropriate behaviour.

SAND CAN HURT!

Learning objective
To consider the consequences of their words and actions for themselves and others.

What you need
Two hand puppets; sand; sand tray; sand equipment, such as a spade, fork, scoop and bucket.

Preparation
Put the equipment into a tray of sand.

What to do
Ask the children to stand in front of the sand tray and introduce the two hand puppets to them. Make up the voices of the puppets, greeting the children and telling them that the puppets are playing in the sand today. Manipulate the puppets so that they appear to be playing harmoniously in the sand for a while, before making one of them behave inappropriately, for example, throwing sand over the other puppet. Stop the action and talk to the children about what the puppets were doing. Did they think that it was a good thing to throw the sand? Can they say why not?

Put away the puppets and discuss issues such as sand safety and considering others. Tell the children that there is time for them to play in the sand and ask them to remember the rules that they have discussed as they play.

Support
Talk to younger children about their actions as they are actually playing rather than using the puppets. For example, praise them for sharing equipment and ask them to think about how another child feels if they snatch something from them.

Extension
Encourage older children to consider the needs of younger children, for example, showing them how to use a sand wheel and helping them to put things away in the right place.

Emotional
development

• • • • • •

4 Responds to
significant
experiences,
showing a range of
feelings when
appropriate.

• • • • • •

9 Displays a strong
and positive sense
of self-identity and
is able to express a
range of emotions
fluently and
appropriately.

GROUP SIZE
Up to eight
children.

TIMING
20 minutes.

ASSESSMENT

Does the child show a range of
feelings in response to the music played?

Does he or she talk confidently about likes and
dislikes, for example, preferences for certain types
of music? (4)

Does he or she express emotions such as joy or
anxiety easily, and control emotions such as anger in
appropriate ways? (9)

HOME LINKS

Invite parents and
carers to listen to,
and share their
feelings about, a
range of different
music with their
children.

MUSICAL EMOTIONS

Learning objective
To respond to significant experiences, showing a range of feelings when appropriate.

What you need
Recordings of music to reflect different moods, such as *The William Tell Overture* by Rossini (excited), *Radetzky March* by Strauss (happy), *Air on a G String* by Bach (dreamy/sad); tape recorder or CD player.

Preparation
Record short sections or note track numbers for the selected music beforehand.

What to do
Invite the children to sit or lie on the carpet so that they can listen to some music in comfort. Explain that they might enjoy the music more if they close their eyes.

Begin by playing a slow, dreamy piece, such as *Air on a G String*. Ask the children whether they liked the music. How did it make them feel?

Play a rousing piece, such as *Radetzky March*. Does this music make them feel the same as the previous one? What was different about it? Play the music again and suggest that the children move freely around the room if they wish to.

Ask the children to move back into their relaxed positions and play another piece of music. Continue to explore the music while the children remain motivated.

Support
Younger children may be upset by loud or rousing music. Be aware of this and adjust the volume or choice of music accordingly. Encourage them to respond through body movements if they do not have the language skills to talk about how the music makes them feel.

Extension
Leave a tape recorder and recordings of contrasting music on a carpet space so that older children can play music and respond by either listening quietly or making up their own dance movements.

CHAPTER 2

Provide opportunities to evaluate the children's skills by encouraging them to use speaking, reading and writing effectively in their play.

Communication, language and literacy

FOUNDATION STAGE PROFILE LINKS
Language for communication and thinking

• • • • • •

1 Listens and responds.

• • • • • •

4 Listens with enjoyment to stories, songs, rhymes and poems, sustains attentive listening and responds with relevant comments, questions or actions.

• • • • • •

9 Talks and listens confidently and with control, consistently showing awareness of the listener by including relevant detail.

GROUP SIZE
Up to eight children.

TIMING
20 minutes.

HOME LINKS
Invite parents and carers to read a variety of stories to their children and to encourage them to join in.

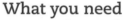

LET'S HEAR IT AGAIN!

Learning objective
To listen with enjoyment, and respond to stories, songs and other music, rhymes and poems and make up their own stories, songs, rhymes and poems.

ASSESSMENT
Does the child listen to what others say and respond through words and gestures? (1)

Does the child listen attentively and with enjoyment as the stories are read? Can the child recall detail within the story, for example, when discussing favourite characters or answering questions about the sequence of events? (4)

Does the child listen attentively in other situations, such as group discussions, and talk confidently, showing an awareness of the listener by altering the tone of voice or vocabulary used? (9)

What you need
A copy of one of the children's favourite stories; portable tape recorder; blank tape.

Preparation
Using the portable tape recorder, record a member of staff reading some of the children's favourite stories.

What to do
Invite the children to choose a favourite story from a wide selection. Read the chosen story aloud to the children and encourage them to join in with repeated phrases and to anticipate sentence endings.

Play the children the recorded version of the story. Explain that you will put the tape in the story corner, along with recordings of other favourite stories, for them to play by themselves later.

Ask for volunteers to retell the story in their own words, either individually or in pairs.

Encourage the children to visit the story corner and play the recordings. Ensure that copies of the books are also available.

Support
Choose shorter stories for younger children, with lots of repetition so that they can join in with confidence.

Extension
Encourage older children to make up stories of their own and to use the portable tape recorder to record these to play back to their friends.

LET'S VISIT THE HAIR SALON

Learning objective

To use language to imagine and re-create roles and experiences.

What you need

Three screens; two small square tables; low rectangular table; home-corner sink unit; four small chairs; safety mirrors; towels; hairbrushes; combs; rollers; hair ornaments such as slides and clips; empty shampoo and conditioner bottles; empty water spray bottle; telephone; till; notepad; diary; pencils; two tabards; magazines about hair care.

Preparation

Set up a role-play hair salon. Enclose the area with the three screens and use one of the small square tables for the receptionist and the other as a styling table, housing the mirrors. Position two chairs at the tables and two near to the entrance for waiting customers. Have a low table in front of the waiting customers, with magazines about hair care displayed on it.

Arrange the rest of the resources appropriately, for example, the towels and bottles on the sink unit and the hair ornaments on the styling table.

Wash resources such as hairbrushes, combs and hair ornaments frequently to prevent infection.

ASSESSMENT

Does the child talk and listen with greater self-confidence in informal contexts, rather than in structured activities such as circle time? (2)

Does the child use language during role-play and other informal contexts, to imagine, re-create and develop experiences? (5)

What to do

Show the children the hair salon and invite them to recall their own experiences of having their hair styled. Did they visit a hair salon or have their hair cut at home?

Suggest to the children that they decide on roles, for example, a hair stylist, receptionist and two customers. Invite the 'staff' to put on tabards. Interact in the play initially, to encourage the children to communicate effectively. Emphasise the function of the telephone to book appointments to stimulate imaginary language further.

Support

Ensure that younger children are comfortable in this role-play situation, as some might be reluctant to have their hair touched.

Extension

Encourage older children to develop their use of imaginary language by suggesting specific situations, such as styling hair for a bridal party.

BUILDING IN MINIATURE

Learning objective
To use talk to organise, sequence and clarify thinking, ideas, feelings and events.

What you need
Recycled items such as boxes, tubes, card, paper and cartons; tape; glue; scissors; small-world characters.

Preparation
Set up a recycling system to collect appropriate resources.

What to do
Show the children the small-world characters and suggest that they make houses for them, from the selection of recycled materials. Invite the children to work in pairs and ask each pair to choose a family of small-world characters to build a house for.

Encourage the children to talk about how they will build the house by asking them appropriate questions. Will they use one large box or several smaller boxes? How will they join the boxes together? Will it be a bungalow or have different storeys? What rooms will they include? Will the characters share a bedroom or have a bedroom each?

When the houses are finished, ask each couple of children to explain to the rest of the group how they made their house.

Support
Invite younger children to choose one box to use as the house in which to play with the characters. Include some plastic furniture. Encourage them to talk about what the characters are doing in the house, for example, eating, sleeping and playing.

Extension
Challenge older children by asking them to create furniture, curtains and carpets from recycled items such as cotton reels, wood offcuts and fabric scraps. Invite them to talk about their ideas and how they decided on the resources that they have used.

FOUNDATION STAGE PROFILE LINKS

Language for communication and thinking

• • • • • •

7 Uses talk to organise, sequence and clarify thinking, ideas, feelings and events, exploring the meanings and sounds of new words.

• • • • • •

9 Uses language to work out and clarify ideas, showing control of a range of appropriate vocabulary.

GROUP SIZE
Up to six children.

TIMING
Ten to 15 minutes.

ASSESSMENT
Is the child beginning to use language rather than action, talking either alone or to others when reflecting on actions that he or she is carrying out? (7)

Does the child use language to clarify ideas, and demonstrate a good range of appropriate vocabulary? (9)

HOME LINKS
Suggest to parents or carers that they present their children with simple problems during play by asking appropriate questions. Emphasise the importance of encouraging their children to explain verbally how they solve problems.

PICKING UP SPEED

Learning objective
To use talk to organise, sequence and clarify thinking, ideas, feelings and events.

What you need
Small vehicles; strips of thick card; short planks; wooden blocks of differing heights; slide.

What to do
Invite the children to spend a few minutes going up and down a slide. What happens to their bodies when they sit at the top? Explain to them that a slope like the one on the slide is sometimes called a ramp and suggest that they create ramps for some small vehicles. Can they think of how they might make them?

Supply the children with differing lengths of thick card, short planks and a selection of wooden blocks and invite them to make slopes of differing gradients. Encourage the children to share their observations and ideas with the rest of the group and to work together.

Once the ramps are completed, allow time for the children to play with the vehicles, exploring whether speed and distance travelled varies with gradients.

Ask the children to take turns to talk about how they made the ramps, explaining their actions in the correct sequence.

Support
Help younger children to make the ramps and encourage them to talk about what they are doing. Introduce new vocabulary to support their descriptions.

Extension
Pose problems to challenge older children, for example, ask them to make a gradient steeper and invite them to explain to others how they solved the problem.

Language for communication and thinking

• • • • • •

8 Speaks clearly with confidence and control, showing awareness of the listener.

• • • • • •

9 Talks and listens confidently and with control, consistently showing awareness of the listener by including relevant detail.

GROUP SIZE
Up to 12 children.

TIMING
Ten minutes.

TRAVELLING TOYS

Learning objective
To speak clearly and audibly with confidence and control and show awareness of the listener.

What you need
A soft toy or doll; set of day and night clothes for the toy; small case; diary or notebook; pencil; small blanket; small toothbrush.

Preparation
Dress the chosen toy in day clothes and pack the case.

What to do
Introduce the toy to the children and show them the contents of the case. Explain that the toy has packed a holiday case and suggest to the children that they take turns to take the toy home for the weekend.

Draw up a list of children to take home the toy, along with the dates, and display this on the wall. Show the children the diary and invite them to fill it in with their parents or carers over the weekend.

When a child returns with the toy, read the diary and ask the child to tell the others about what has happened. Emphasise that the others must listen carefully to what is being said.

ASSESSMENT
Is the child able to use language to reflect on experiences, for example, when talking about events enjoyed by the toy at the weekend? Does he or she organise his or her thoughts logically, for example, following events in sequence? (8)

Does the child demonstrate an awareness of the listener, for example, by explaining in greater detail events that took place away from the setting? Does he or she include new vocabulary related to the events? (9)

Support
Help younger children to recall the toy's adventures by asking simple questions as you read the diary, for example, 'Lucky Jake went to tea at Granny's with you. What did you have to eat?'.

Extension
Encourage older children to collect souvenirs to put into the case, such as a cinema ticket, and ask them to talk about them.

HOME LINKS
Involve parents and carers in the activity by asking them to care for the toy and fill in the diary.

TIME FOR A RHYME

Learning objective
To hear and say initial and final sounds in words, and short vowel sounds within words.

What you need
Props related to the children's favourite rhymes, such as a toy black sheep and three small bags stuffed with cotton wool for the traditional rhyme 'Baa, Baa, Black Sheep'; drawstring bags; card labels.

Preparation
Put the props associated with each rhyme into a bag and attach a label to the top indicating the rhyme.

What to do
Ask the children to sit around the bags and invite one of them to take something out of one of them. Can the children guess which rhyme the object represents?

Say the rhyme together, then ask the children to listen while you say it alone, emphasising the rhyming words. Next, say the rhyming words in isolation, for example, 'wool' and 'full'. Talk about how the words sound the same, and introduce the word 'rhyme'.

Explain that you have made up a song of your own by changing one of the words in a favourite rhyme, for example:

'Hickory, dickory, dock,
The mouse ran up the chair.'

Does this new song rhyme? Create another version, this time rhyming:

'Hickory, dickory, dock,
The mouse ran up the sock.'

Which version do the children prefer?

Invite the children to make up their own nonsense songs based on their favourite rhymes.

Support
Say familiar nursery rhymes slowly and clearly to younger children, with emphasis on rhyming words, and encourage the children to join in or move to the rhythm.

Extension
Encourage older children to become aware of initial sounds by making up nonsense strings of words, such as a menu containing sweet sausages, chilly chips and peppermint peas.

FOUNDATION STAGE PROFILE LINKS

Linking sounds and letters

• • • • • •

3 Links some sounds to letters.

• • • • • •

4 Links sounds to letters, naming and sounding letters of the alphabet.

GROUP SIZE

Four children.

TIMING

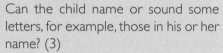

20 minutes.

SOUND BOOKS

Learning objective

To link sounds to letters, naming and sounding the letters of the alphabet.

What you need

Mail-order and early years catalogues; magazines; sugar paper; textured scraps, such as fake fur, sandpaper and thin sponge; PVA glue; scissors; felt-tipped pens; string.

Preparation

Create a large book from sugar paper, fastening the sheets together by punching holes down the centre and threading string through them. Include a string loop to hang the book up.

What to do

Show the children the empty book and suggest that they fill the pages with pictures of objects starting with the same letter sound.

Choose a letter sound together and ask the children to look through the catalogues and magazines for appropriate pictures. Invite them to cut out their favourite pictures and glue them into the book. Write the names of the objects under the pictures, scribing for the children if necessary.

Fill in the spaces on the pages by asking the children to draw things starting with the chosen letter. Create a large letter with a textured surface, such as sandpaper or sponge, for the front of the book, so that the children can feel the shape.

Make other books in the same way, focusing on other letters and with a different texture on the front. Hang the books in the graphics area or book corner.

ASSESSMENT

Can the child name or sound some letters, for example, those in his or her name? (3)

Does the child recognise the letters of the alphabet, and is he or she able to name and sound most of them? (4)

HOME LINKS

Invite parents and carers to play games such as 'I spy' with their children and ask them to bring in objects with the same initial sound for a 'Letter of the week' table.

Support

Cut some pictures out beforehand, all starting with the focused letter, and ask younger children to choose a picture to stick in the book. Say the word and emphasise the initial letter as you do so.

Extension

Make some small books from sheets of folded paper and leave these in the graphics area along with plastic letters and pictures of different objects to encourage older children to make their own alphabet books.

FOUNDATION STAGE PROFILE LINKS

Linking sounds and letters

● ● ● ● ● ●

5 Hears and says initial and final sounds in words.

● ● ● ● ● ●

6 Hears and says short vowel sounds within words.

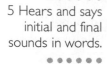

GROUP SIZE
Six children.

TIMING
15 to 20 minutes.

ASSESSMENT

Is the child able to distinguish and say the initial and final sounds in a word? (5)

Can the child identify some short vowel sounds in the middle of a word with letters in a 'cvc' arrangement? (6)

SOUND IT OUT!

Learning objective

To hear and say initial and final sounds in words, and short vowel sounds within words.

What you need

A selection of objects, each with three letters in their name in the order 'consonant, vowel, consonant' ('cvc'), for example, a hat, pen, bag and toy cat; card; felt-tipped pen.

Preparation

Cut the card into rectangles and write the name of one of the objects on each card in large lower-case letters.

What to do

Ask the children to sit in a circle with the objects in the centre and the cards in a pile, face-down, alongside them. Invite the children to take turns to pick up a card from the pile and read out the letter sounds in order. Can they say the word? Once the group has agreed on the word, invite the child to find the object from the selection in the circle.

Talk about the object and ask the children to say the word slowly. Can they tell you which is the first sound that they say? Which is the last sound? Can they decide which sound is in the middle of the word? Invite the rest of the group to help.

Continue to take turns to turn over cards and read them until all of the objects have been picked up.

Support

Invite younger children to choose an object rather than read a card, then concentrate on saying the word and emphasising the initial sound.

Extension

Invite older children to choose one of the objects, then give instructions based on letter sounds, for example, 'Hold up your object if it starts with "c"', 'Put your object back in the circle if it ends with "d"' or 'Who has an object with "a" in the middle?'.

HOME LINKS
Explain the activity to parents and carers and ask them to talk about the initial sounds of family names.

FOUNDATION STAGE PROFILE LINKS

Linking sounds and letters

● ● ● ● ● ●

7 Uses phonic knowledge to read simple regular words.

● ● ● ● ● ●

8 Attempts to read more complex words, using phonic knowledge.

GROUP SIZE
Four children.

TIMING
Ten to 15 minutes.

ASSESSMENT
Does the child use his or her phonic knowledge to read simple words, for example, those on the picture display in the activity? (7)

Does the child attempt to read more complex words and sometimes seek support from adults? (8)

HOME LINKS
Encourage parents and carers to help their children to read words around them, for example, in supermarkets.

READ AND CHECK

Learning objective
To link sounds to letters, naming and sounding the letters of the alphabet.

What you need
Pictures of objects, each with three letters in their name in the order 'cvc', for example, a hat, pen and toy cat; card; felt-tipped pen; board; Velcro; tape; scissors; ribbon; pencils; crayons; paper; glue.

Preparation
Cut out the pictures of objects and glue them on to card. Attach a matching piece of card with tape along the edge of each card above the picture, to form a lift-up flap that conceals the picture when the flap is down. Write the appropriate word on top of the flap in lower-case letters. Attach a strip of ribbon to the base so that the children can lift it.

Display the covered pictures on a low board and attach a small strip of Velcro below each one. Create a set of cards with the words of the objects written clearly in lower-case letters. Attach a small strip of Velcro to the back of each one. Leave pencils, crayons and paper alongside the display.

What to do
Invite the children to lift the flaps and talk about the pictures that are showing underneath. Next, ask them to take turns to read a word, and then to lift the flap to check if they are correct.

Introduce a matching set of words with Velcro attached to the back of each card. Invite the children to match the words on these cards to those on the flaps and to attach them to the Velcro underneath.

Allow time for the children to play freely with the resources, including the writing materials.

Support
Supply younger children with a set of matching pictures to attach, rather than word cards.

Extension
Encourage older children to attempt to write their own words using the materials alongside the display.

FOUNDATION STAGE PROFILE LINKS
Linking sounds and letters

• • • • • •

9 Uses knowledge of letters, sounds and words when reading and writing independently.

GROUP SIZE
Four children.

TIMING
20 minutes.

ASSESSMENT
Does the child make use of his or her developing knowledge of letters, sounds and words when reading and writing independently, for example, to create his or her own story-books?

HOME LINKS
Suggest to parents and carers that they encourage their children to write their own messages on postcards, greetings cards and letters to family members and friends.

BUDDING AUTHORS

Learning objective
To use their phonic knowledge to write simple regular words and make phonetically plausible attempts at more complex words.

What you need
Favourite story-books; small doll; plain white paper; sugar paper; crayons; pencils; stapler; glue.

Preparation
Make small books of varying sizes from two sheets of paper folded in half and stapled down the centre fold. Create the outside sheet from sugar paper to strengthen the book. Cut out some small white pieces of paper to stick to the front of each book.

What to do
Read one of the children's favourite stories to them and talk about the main character. Show the children the doll and suggest that they make up some stories of their own about the doll's adventures.

Begin by asking the children to draw a picture of the doll on a small piece of paper to stick to the front cover. While the children are drawing, talk to each one in turn about the story that they would like to tell. Can they think of a name for the doll? How would they write this word?

Support them as necessary as they attempt the letters. Write very short sentences on each page for the children, asking questions about the letters that you will need to form the words. Ask if they would like to write some words for themselves and suggest that they illustrate each page.

Display the children's books in the story corner and encourage them to 'read' them to their friends.

Support
Make books for younger children from one sheet of paper folded in half and ask them to draw a picture in the centre. Write a short caption for them about the picture that they have drawn.

Extension
Make sure that there are blank books available in the graphics area so that older children can attempt to write their own stories.

FOUNDATION
STAGE PROFILE
LINKS
Reading

• • • • • •

1 Is developing an
interest in books.

• • • • • •

9 Reads books of
own choice with
some fluency and
accuracy.

GROUP SIZE
Four children.

TIMING
Ten to 15 minutes.

ASSESSMENT
Does the child enjoy looking at books
in the role-play library? Does he or she
handle them appropriately, holding
them the right way up, turning the pages and talking
about the content? (1)

Does the child attempt to read some of the words
in the books, and seek help with unfamiliar or more
difficult words? (9)

A LIBRARY OF OUR OWN

Learning objective
To show an understanding of the elements of stories, such as main character, sequence of events, and openings, and how information can be found in non-fiction texts to answer questions about where, who, why and how.

What you need
A selection of fiction and non-fiction books appropriate to the age range and interests of the children; book shelves; screens; book box; small chairs; floor cushions; overall; small table; plastic ice scraper; string; rubber date stamp; telephone; notepad; pencil; posters about reading and books; set of the children's name cards with space for date stamps; wall hanging with pockets; soft toys.

Preparation
Ask a lending library or bookshop to provide you with suitable posters to put up in your role-play library. Tie a length of string to a plastic ice scraper to create a 'scanner'. Create a child-size librarian's overall from a larger one and arrange the book shelves and screens to enclose the area.

What to do
Talk to the children about their library experiences and suggest that they set up their own library.

Arrange the book box, seating, soft toys and floor cushions in the area. Attach the posters and wall hanging to the screens and set up the librarian's table. Display fiction and non-fiction books separately on the shelves and in the book box.

As the children play, demonstrate how to borrow a book by having it 'scanned', and how to hand in a name card to be stamped and scanned before putting it into a pocket on the wall hanging.

Leave the library open for other children to visit.

Support
Visit the library with younger children after it has been organised. Read their chosen books and talk about their choices.

Extension
Encourage older children to find books related to your current topic.

HOME LINKS
Encourage parents
and carers to take
their children to visit
a local library.

ASSESSMENT

Can the child distinguish between pictures and print? Does he or she realise that print carries meaning? (2)

Does the child follow the print from left to right and top to bottom, for example, when following the text on the page of a big book? (4)

POINT IT OUT

Learning objective
To know that print carries meaning and, in English, is read from left to right and top to bottom.

What you need
A copy of a favourite big book, such as *Rumble in the Jungle* by Giles Andreae (Orchard Books); book stand or easel; pointer or short piece of dowelling.

What to do
Invite the children to sit in front of the book stand and display the closed book on it. Discuss the title of the story and the names of the author and illustrator (David Wojtowycz).

Read the story to the children and point to the words with a finger as you read.

Read the story again, this time inviting individual children to answer questions about it. Suggest that they might like to use the pointer instead of a finger to point things out. Start at the front of the book and invite a child to point to the title of the book and the author's name. Ask other children to point out a word, letter or object in the picture.

Talk about where the story starts and finishes and use words such as 'page', 'cover', 'front', 'back' and 'turn over' during your discussions.

Support
Invite younger children to point to something that they like on the picture and talk about how the words tell us more about it, for example, 'Well done, you have pointed to the little dog. It says here that the little dog was looking for someone to play with. Shall we turn over and see if she finds someone?'.

Extension
Invite older children to turn over the pages and to tell you what they think the words might say as they move a finger along them.

FOUNDATION STAGE PROFILE LINKS
Reading

● ● ● ● ● ●

3 Recognises a few familiar words.

● ● ● ● ● ●

6 Reads a range of familiar and common words and simple sentences independently.

GROUP SIZE
Four children.

TIMING
Ten to 15 minutes.

ASSESSMENT
Is the child able to recognise some familiar words, for example, his or her name or words related to objects found in play areas? (3)

Can the child read a range of familiar and common words and simple sentences independently, for example, in a familiar environment? (6)

HOME LINKS
Encourage parents and carers to point out words and simple sentences in the environment, for example, on a shopping trip.

WORD HUNT

Learning objective
To read a range of familiar and common words and simple sentences independently.

What you need
Card; scissors; glue stick; early years catalogue; felt-tipped pen; hole-punch; string; plastic hooks.

Preparation
Find pictures in an early years catalogue of objects that you have in your play areas, such as a plastic cup, doll and pencil. Cut these out and mount them on card. Write the object name under the picture. Create a set of matching cards with words and no pictures. Punch holes in these cards and form a hanging loop with string.

Attach plastic hooks to screens or walls in relevant play areas and hang up the word cards that you have made, for example, the word 'cup' in the home area.

What to do
Show the children the picture cards and ask them to choose one. Talk about the objects on the cards and what the words might say. Ask the children in which play areas they think the objects could be found. Go to one of the areas and ask the child with the relevant picture card to search for the same word. When the child finds the word, ask the other children if they think it matches the word on the picture card.

Continue to visit play areas until all the children have found their matching cards. Sit on the carpet in a group and look at the words together. Play games involving matching the cards.

Support
Create matching cards with words written under pictures for younger children to find. Point to the words afterwards and talk about how they look the same.

Extension
Challenge older children to attempt to read the word first and then check by looking at the picture on the back of a card. Encourage them to try to read short captions around the room.

FOUNDATION STAGE PROFILE LINKS
Reading

• • • • • •

5 Shows an understanding of the elements of stories, such as main character, sequence of events and openings.

• • • • • •

7 Retells narratives in the correct sequence, drawing on language patterns of stories.

GROUP SIZE
Up to six children.

TIMING
20 minutes.

ASSESSMENT
Is the child able to identify the main character and the sequence of events in the chosen story? Does he or she realise that these elements are to be found in most stories? (5)

Is the child able to retell the main points of the story in the correct sequence? Does he or she use appropriate story language, such as 'Once upon a time'? (7)

HOME LINKS
Invite parents and carers to encourage their children to think more about the stories that they read to them by discussing the characters, making comparisons with their own experiences, predicting possible outcomes and suggesting alternative endings.

STORY-TELLERS

Learning objective
To retell narratives in the correct sequence, drawing on language patterns of stories.

What you need
A drawstring bag or pillowcase; props associated with a favourite story, for example, for 'The Gingerbread Man' (Traditional), you could include a rolling-pin, a salt-dough gingerbread man, a male and female doll, and a soft-toy cat, dog, cow and fox; copy of the story.

Preparation
Put the items associated with the story in the drawstring bag.

What to do
Invite the children to sit in a circle and tip out the contents of the bag into the centre. Can the children identify the story? Tell or read the story, holding up the props as you do so.

Suggest that the children take turns to retell the story using the props. Encourage them to use appropriate story language, such as 'Once upon a time', and talk about what happens at the beginning, middle and end of the story. Introduce the word 'character' and name the main character and other characters in the order that they appear.

Support
Tell the story with younger children, pulling the first object of the bag and passing it to a child to hold. Give the next object to the child sitting alongside and continue in this way around the circle. Tell the story again, using the order of the objects around the circle to help the children to decide on the sequence of events.

Extension
Invite older children to re-enact the story and use it as a basis for imaginative role-play and small-world play.

FOUNDATION STAGE PROFILE LINKS
Reading

8 Shows an understanding of how information can be found in non-fiction texts to answer questions about where, who, why and how.

GROUP SIZE
Four children.

TIMING
Ten minutes for initial discussion; 20 minutes at the library.

ASSESSMENT
Does the child understand the difference between fiction and non-fiction books? Is he or she beginning to discover how to find information within non-fiction books, for example, using a contents page or index?

FINDING OUT THE FACTS

Learning objective
To show an understanding of how information can be found in non-fiction texts to answer questions about where, who, why and how.

What you need
Paper; pencil; bag for each child.

Preparation
Set up a display related to a chosen topic, for example, 'Toys', and invite the children to contribute to it.

What to do
Talk to the children about their display and discuss anything else that they would like to know about their chosen topic. For example, they might have displayed lots of their own toys but have little information about toys with which their parents and grandparents played.

Make a list of things that the children would like to know, for example, 'What did old-fashioned dolls' houses look like?'. Explain that the things that they need to know can be found in books, and suggest a visit to a library to look at some. (If you cannot visit a library, use any information books that you have, invite a librarian to visit, or look on the Internet if you have access.)

Take the children, along with their list of questions and a bag each, to the library. Encourage them to ask the librarian their questions, and invite the librarian to show them where and how to find the answers in appropriate reference books. Spend time looking through the books and choose a selection to borrow. Ask the children to carry them back in their bags.

Support
Encourage younger children to look at a selection of books related to an appropriate topic, for example, 'Animals', in your setting. Talk about and name the animals that they point to.

Extension
Take older children to the library on a regular basis and use your own information books, or computer, to discover more about subjects of their choice, for example, 'Dinosaurs' or 'Space'.

HOME LINKS
Suggest to parents and carers that they use books, other reference materials and computers to help their children to answer their questions.

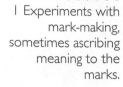

WHAT'S ON THE MENU?

Learning objective
To attempt writing for different purposes, using features of different forms such as lists, stories and instructions.

What you need
Three screens; two small tables; three small chairs; table-cloth; larger table; plastic food, dishes, cups and plates; apron; chef's hat; two customers' hats; till; toy money; telephone; notepad; pencil; card; felt-tipped pen; storage box.

Preparation
Screen off the proposed café area and put a small table covered with a cloth in the centre. Position another small table near to the entrance to house the till, telephone and writing materials. Leave the costumes in a storage box alongside. Put plastic food, dishes, cups and plates on the larger table at the back of the area to represent the kitchen.

ASSESSMENT

Does the child make use of a variety of resources to make marks? Does he or she sometimes give meaning to the marks? (1)

Is the child beginning to write recognisable letters, perhaps some of those in his or her name, and giving meaning to the marks even if the sounds and symbols do not match? (2)

Does the child hold a pencil correctly and use it effectively to form recognisable letters, most of which are correctly formed? (5)

What to do
Explain to the children that you have organised a café for them to play in, but that you did not have time to make menus for customers.

Scribe the children's menu suggestions in clear lower-case letters and put this menu card on the café table. Leave a supply of card and pencils alongside the till so that the children can write their own menus.

Allow time for the children to play freely, taking on the roles of waiter, chef and customers. Invite them to read their menus out to you.

Support
Encourage younger children to create pictorial menus by drawing their chosen food.

Extension
Challenge older children to write down orders and issue receipts to customers as they play.

FOUNDATION
STAGE PROFILE
LINKS

FOUNDATION STAGE PROFILE LINKS
Writing

● ● ● ● ● ●

3 Represents some sounds correctly in writing.

● ● ● ● ● ●

7 Uses phonic knowledge to write simple regular words and make phonetically plausible attempts at more complex words.

GROUP SIZE
Four children.

TIMING
20 minutes.

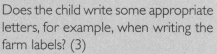

ASSESSMENT
Does the child write some appropriate letters, for example, when writing the farm labels? (3)

Does the child make use of developing phonic knowledge to write simple regular words, such as 'pig', and make phonetically plausible attempts at more complex words, such as 'caw' (cow)? (7)

HOME LINKS
Encourage parents and carers to try a similar activity with their children at home, for example, making family place names for a dolls' tea party.

DOWN ON THE FARM

Learning objective
To use their phonic knowledge to write simple regular words and make phonetically plausible attempts at more complex words.

What you need
Small-world farm buildings and fences; toy farm animals; small tractors and trailers; card; felt-tipped pens; clear tape.

Preparation
Cut the card into small rectangles, measuring approximately 6cm x 3cm, to make labels.

What to do
Work with the children to set out the farm buildings and create enclosures with the fences. Decide which animals will go into the different enclosures and buildings, making sure that there is a designated place for each type of animal.

Explain to the children that there are no animals on this farm yet, as it is a new farm. The farmer has just bought the stock at the local market and they will be delivered by trailer the next day. How will the farmer know where the children have decided to put the animals? What might happen if the farmer puts pigs, sheep and cows in the same field?

Suggest that the enclosures and buildings could be labelled in some way to help the farmer. Sort the animals into groups and create a label for each type.

Encourage the children to help with spelling the words. Once the labels have been written, tape them to the correct enclosures or buildings.

Fill the trailers with animals of the same type and deliver them to the farm, making several journeys if necessary.

Support
Invite younger children to draw pictures of the animals on larger labels and write the words underneath for them.

Extension
Leave some card, tape and pens along with the rest of the resources to encourage older children to create more labels of their own.

FOUNDATION STAGE PROFILE LINKS
Writing
• • • • • •
4 Writes own name and other words from memory.

GROUP SIZE
Four children.

TIMING
Ten to 15 minutes for the activity; time for a shopping trip.

ASSESSMENT
Is the child able to write his or her first name and some words of personal importance, for example, the names of family members?

HOME LINKS
Suggest to parents and carers that they involve their children in writing shopping lists and entrust them with ticking off purchases during shopping visits.

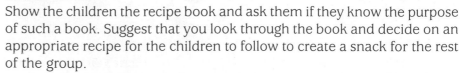

TIME FOR SOME SHOPPING

Learning objective
To write their own names and other things such as labels and captions.

What you need
A recipe book; paper; pencils.

What to do
Show the children the recipe book and ask them if they know the purpose of such a book. Suggest that you look through the book and decide on an appropriate recipe for the children to follow to create a snack for the rest of the group.

Read out the ingredients for your chosen recipe, pointing to the words with a finger as you do so. As you read each item look and see whether you have it in stock or whether you will need to buy it.

Suggest that you write a shopping list of the things that you need, as well as the quantities. Write the list as the children watch, sounding out the words as you do so and reading each one again after you have written it.

Ask the children how they might share out the task of purchasing the ingredients and suggest that each take responsibility for purchasing one of the items. Invite each child to write down the chosen item on a piece of paper. Consider together how the children will know which is their piece of paper and suggest that they write their names at the top.

Go for a shopping trip to purchase the ingredients, with the children carrying their own pieces of paper. At the shop invite the children to read out what they have written and look for the items together.

Follow the activity by leaving paper and pencils in the home area for the children to write their own shopping lists.

Support
Supply younger children with large name cards so that they can attempt to write some of the letters in their names during mark-making activities and role-play.

Extension
Encourage older children to write messages and reminders, and to include their names, as part of imaginative play.

FOUNDATION STAGE PROFILE LINKS
Writing

• • • • • •

6 Attempts writing for a variety of purposes, using features of different forms.

GROUP SIZE
Up to six children.

TIMING
Ten to 15 minutes.

ASSESSMENT
Does the child attempt writing for different purposes, for example, when making birthday cards and party invitations for his or her friends?

HAPPY BIRTHDAY TO YOU!

Learning objective
To attempt writing for different purposes, using features of different forms such as lists, stories and instructions.

What you need
Card; scissors; glue; old birthday cards; foil numbers representing the ages of the children in the group; pencils; name cards; shoebox; birthday wrapping paper.

Preparation
Cut the card into rectangles a suitable size for greetings cards.

What to do
Look at the old birthday cards and invite the children to make some new cards to give to those who are celebrating birthdays. Show them the prepared blank cards and ask them what needs to be added to make them into birthday cards.

Ask each child to choose pictures from the old cards to cut out. Talk about which is the front, back and middle of a blank card. Where will the children stick their pictures? What else might they put on the front of the card? Show them the numbers and invite them to add one if they wish.

Look at the writing on the old birthday cards. Point out familiar words such as 'Happy birthday' and 'Many happy returns'. Help each child to write their chosen words on the cover of their card.

Turn to the inside of each card and write 'From (*child's name*) and the rest of your friends'. Invite the children to write their names and some of the words if they are able.

Cover a shoebox with birthday wrapping paper to house the cards. Invite children who are celebrating their birthday to choose a card at circle time.

HOME LINKS
Suggest to parents and carers that they ask their children to help write greetings cards for family and friends, for example, by writing their name and the name of the recipient.

Support
Cut out the pictures for younger children and invite them to choose one or two to stick to the card. Write the words for them and encourage them to make a mark, such as a kiss, underneath.

Extension
Encourage older children to recognise and write some of the repeated words, such as 'Happy birthday' and 'Love from', and to write their names from memory.

ALL ABOUT ME

Learning objective

To write their own names and other things such as labels and captions and begin to form simple sentences, sometimes using punctuation.

What you need

Sugar paper; white paper; personal photographs; glue sticks; crayons; felt-tipped pens; pencils.

Preparation

Put up a notice explaining that the children are making books about themselves, inviting parents and carers to send in photographs and personal mementoes, such as birthday cards or holiday postcards, to include in the books.

Create some blank books using white paper for the pages and sugar paper for the cover.

What to do

Include this activity as part of a topic on 'All about me'. Suggest that the children might like to make a special book about themselves to show to their friends and family.

Discuss with the children what they might include in the book and plan out different sections or 'chapters', for example, 'My family', 'My toys' and 'My holidays'.

Tackle one section at a time and encourage the children to draw pictures, attach photographs and mementoes, and write simple captions. Scribe for the children where necessary.

As you are working together, talk to the children about the words on each page. Introduce appropriate vocabulary, such as 'word' and 'sentence'. Point out simple punctuation, for example, full stops and capital letters.

Support

Talk to younger children about the things that they put on a page and explain that you are writing 'words' about their pictures and photographs. Read the words to them.

Extension

Encourage older children to be involved in as much of the writing of their books as they are able, giving lots of positive praise for their attempts and supporting them in their efforts.

CHAPTER 3

Plan activities using numbers as labels and for counting, calculating, and shape, space and measures, and use these as opportunities to assess the children's skills in this Area of Learning.

Mathematical development

FOUNDATION
STAGE PROFILE
LINKS

FOUNDATION STAGE PROFILE LINKS

Numbers as labels and for counting

• • • • • •

1 Says some number names in familiar contexts, such as nursery rhymes.

• • • • • •

4 Says number names in order.

• • • • • •

7 Orders numbers, up to 10.

GROUP SIZE
Up to ten children.

TIMING
Ten minutes.

TEN GREEN BOTTLES

Learning objective
To say and use number names in order in familiar contexts.

What you need
Green plastic bottles; yellow paper; PVA glue; scissors; large sponge or plastic bricks.

Preparation
Cut out large numerals from 1 to 10 using yellow paper and glue a different number on each of the ten green bottles.

What to do
Sing the rhyme 'Ten Green Bottles' (Traditional) and show the children the ten numbered bottles.

Suggest that the children create a brick wall to arrange the bottles on. Ask them to take turns to put a brick on the wall until they are all satisfied with the finished wall. Is the top level? Is it long enough to put ten bottles on top? Adjust the bricks, or add more, if necessary.

Ask a child to find the number '1' bottle and put it on top of the wall. Discuss the position of this first bottle. Where will it need to be to leave room for the other bottles? Continue to choose children to find the bottles in order, challenging older children to find the higher numbers.

Sing the rhyme again and invite the children to go to the wall and knock a numbered green bottle from it. When all the bottles are on the floor, ask the children to put them back again in order.

ASSESSMENT
Does the child join in with number rhymes and sometimes use number names in imaginative play? (1)

Can the child say number names in sequence up to ten, counting up or down, for example, when reciting rhymes or playing dice games? (4)

Can the child arrange numbers in order from 1 to 10, for example, when putting the ten green bottles on the wall? (7)

HOME LINKS

Invite carers to ask their children to say numbers in order as they sing number rhymes.

Support
Sing 'Five green bottles' with younger children, until they are familiar with the names and order of these numbers.

Extension
With older children, sing other number rhymes using props, such as 'Ten Fat Sausages' and 'Ten in the Bed' (both Traditional).

FOUNDATION STAGE PROFILE LINKS

Numbers as labels and for counting

• • • • • •

2 Counts reliably up to 3 everyday objects.

• • • • • •

3 Counts reliably up to 6 everyday objects.

• • • • • •

6 Counts reliably up to 10 everyday objects.

GROUP SIZE

Six children.

TIMING

Ten to 15 minutes.

GRAB AND COUNT

Learning objective
To count reliably up to 10 everyday objects.

What you need
Small objects, such as wooden cubes.

What to do
Ask the children to sit in a circle and put some small objects in a pile in the middle. Explain that you are going to play a counting game with the objects, then invite each child to choose a partner.

Demonstrate how to grab a handful of objects, tip them on the floor, arrange them in a row and count them.

Next, invite one child from each pair to start by grabbing a handful of objects and counting them out. Follow this by asking the child's partner to try to grab the same number of objects, and then to check whether they have succeeded by counting.

Talk about the results of the game. Was it easy to grab the same number of objects? Did the second child grab more or less than the first?

ASSESSMENT
Can the child count up to three objects, or take out a certain number of objects, from a larger group? (2)

Can the child count up to six objects, or take out a certain number of objects, from a larger group? (3)

Can the child count up to ten objects, or take out a certain number of objects, from a larger group? (6)

HOME LINKS

Invite parents and carers to count objects, or take out a required number of objects from a group, with their children, for example, taking two pegs out of a basket or counting a row of pegs on a washing line.

Support
Put just five objects on the floor and invite younger children to try to grab them all at once. Tip the grabbed objects on to the floor and count them together. Always praise the children for their efforts, whether or not they manage to grab all five objects.

Extension
With older children, play the game using balance scales. Ask them to work in pairs, grabbing a handful of objects and putting them on one of the pans. Do the pans balance? Is one heavier? Can they guess why? Count out the objects on each pan.

FOUNDATION STAGE PROFILE LINKS

Numbers as labels and for counting

• • • • • •

5 Recognises numerals 1 to 9.

GROUP SIZE

Four children.

TIMING

20 minutes.

TEN IN THE BED

Learning objective
To recognise numerals 1 to 9.

What you need
A shoebox and its lid; brown paint; pieces of brightly coloured fabric; sponge scraps; ten dolly pegs; scissors; felt-tipped pen; thin string; card.

Preparation
Cut the sponge to form a mattress and a long pillow to fit into the shoebox. Create bed covers from brightly coloured fabric scraps.

What to do
Sing the song 'Ten in the Bed' (Traditional) and suggest that the children make some dolls and a bed to re-enact the song.

ASSESSMENT
Does the child recognise numerals 1 to 9 consistently, for example, those on the shoebox bed?

Ask two of the children to paint the shoebox with brown paint, while the other two paint the lid. Put the sponge mattress in the bottom of the box and tuck some brightly coloured fabric around it. Do the same with the pillow, along the long edge of the box.

Show the children the pegs and invite them to create dolls by dressing the pegs with fabric scraps tied on with string. Ask them to draw on the dolls' features with felt-tipped pens.

Write numerals from 1 to 10 along the top of the inside of the lid and glue it upright against the back of the 'bed'. Explain that each doll has a numbered place in the bed.

Put the dolls into bed and cover them with fabric bed covers. Cut down the short sides of the box to the level of the mattress so that the dolls can be rolled out.

Sing the rhyme again and take turns to roll a doll from the bed. Say how many are left by reading the numerals. Invite the entire group to check by counting together.

Support
Sing 'Five in the bed' with younger children to encourage them to recognise numerals up to 5.

Extension
Encourage older children to write numerals from 1 to 10 on small squares of card and tie these to the fronts of the dolls. Ask them to match the numerals on the dolls to those on the back of the bed in order to find the correct places for the dolls.

HOME LINKS

Invite parents and carers to point out numerals to their children both indoors and outdoors, for example, on telephones, clocks, buses and cars.

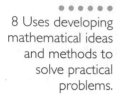

Numbers as labels and for counting

● ● ● ● ● ●

8 Uses developing mathematical ideas and methods to solve practical problems.

GROUP SIZE

ASSESSMENT

Does the child attempt to solve a simple problem, such as sharing out fruit equally, by applying mathematical ideas and methods? Does he or she respond to questions about what to do next, for example, when the pieces of fruit are of different sizes?

ALL EQUAL

Learning objective

To use developing mathematical ideas and methods to solve practical problems.

What you need

Three eating apples; chopping board; knife (adult use).

What to do

Show the children the apples and explain that they are for them to eat but that you want to make sure that they all have the same amount. Start by asking a child to give out the apples to the others. Is there an apple for each child? What about the child who is giving out the apples – does he or she have one? Can the children suggest what to do to make sure that this child has some of the apples, too?

Gather the three apples back in and cut one of them in half. Hand out the pieces so that each child has either a half or a whole apple. Do the children think that they all have the same amount of apple? Can they tell you why not? Can they suggest what to do next, in order for all the children to have the same?

Try cutting another apple in half, and then the last apple. Is it possible to share out the apples? Ask for suggestions from the children and try out their ideas.

If the children do not solve the problem themselves, suggest that they consider cutting the apples into quarters until finally the apples are shared with each child having three quarters of an apple each.

Support

Cut the apples into quarters beforehand and ask younger children to take a piece each, and then another piece. Finally ask them to count to see that they all have the same number of quarters.

Extension

Challenge older children by asking them to cut up pieces of fruit at snack time and share them out equally for the rest of the children.

FOUNDATION STAGE PROFILE LINKS

Numbers as labels and for counting

• • • • • •

9 Recognises, counts, orders and writes numerals up to 20.

GROUP SIZE

Four children.

TIMING

20 minutes.

ASSESSMENT

Does the child understand numbers up to 20, for example, can he or she count and order up to 20 objects, and recognise and write the numbers, generally accurately?

HOME LINKS

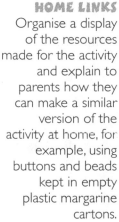

Organise a display of the resources made for the activity and explain to parents how they can make a similar version of the activity at home, for example, using buttons and beads kept in empty plastic margarine cartons.

HOW MANY?

Learning objectives

To count reliably up to 10 everyday objects; to recognise numerals from 1 to 9.

What you need

Ten shallow trays (seed trays are ideal); card; felt-tipped pen; sticky tape; ten different types of small objects, such as cars, toy farm animals and plastic cubes; plastic bucket.

Preparation

Cut out ten card labels and number them from 1 to 10. Ensure that you have ten of each type of object and put them all into a plastic bucket.

What to do

Tip the contents of the bucket on to the floor and ask the children to try to find a certain number of objects, for example, four toy sheep or five plastic cubes.

Discuss how difficult this is when the objects are mixed up and invite the children to sort them into separate containers. Repeat the request for four toy sheep and five cubes. Is it easier to find them when they have been separated?

Explain that you are going to attach number labels to the trays. Empty them and stick a label to the back of each tray. Invite the children to arrange the trays in numerical order and ask them to count out the correct number of objects to put into each tray.

Allow time for the children to play freely with the trays and the selection of small objects.

Support

Fix card 'shadows' to the bottom of the trays so that younger children can match the objects to their shadows. Attach number labels to the backs of the trays and encourage the children to count the number of objects in each tray, but restrict the number of objects to a maximum of five.

Extension

Challenge older children to help to write labels, from 1 to 20, for plastic containers. Ask them to put the correct number of small objects into the containers and to arrange these in order.

FOUNDATION STAGE PROFILE LINKS
Calculating

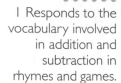

• • • • • •

1 Responds to the vocabulary involved in addition and subtraction in rhymes and games.

GROUP SIZE
Six children.

TIMING
Ten to 15 minutes.

ASSESSMENT

Does the child join in readily when singing number rhymes such as 'Five Currant Buns'? Does he or she use appropriate vocabulary related to addition and subtraction, for example, 'take one away' and 'add one on'?

HOME LINKS
Send home a sheet of number rhymes involving counting down from five or ten, and include directions for actions.

FIVE CURRANT BUNS

Learning objective
In practical activities and discussion to begin to use the vocabulary involved in adding and subtracting.

What you need
Salt dough; red and brown paint; white apron and hat; five plastic 'pennies'; card; low table; tray.

Preparation
Invite the children to make five currant buns from a traditional salt-dough mixture (mix equal quantities of flour and salt with water). Bake the buns slowly until hard and paint currants and a cherry on each bun.

Fold five rectangles of card in half and stand them up with the fold along the top. Write a numeral, from 1 to 5, on each one.

What to do
Invite the children to sing the rhyme 'Five Currant Buns' (Traditional). Display the number cards on a table with the buns on a tray alongside. Count the buns together and put the number '5' card beside them. Choose a child to be the baker, wearing the apron and hat, and give the rest of the children a plastic penny each.

Sing the first verse of the rhyme and choose a child to buy a bun. Ask the baker to exchange the child's penny for a bun, and to put the penny on the table. Count the buns left on the tray and exchange the '5' card for one displaying '4'.

Continue the rhyme, naming children to buy buns, and exchanging coins and cards, until all the buns are sold. Ask the baker to put the pennies in a row as he or she receives them. Use appropriate vocabulary such as 'take one away from the tray' and 'add one to the row'.

Support
Encourage younger children to count during each verse so that they become aware of how the buns are reducing and the coins are increasing.

Extension
Work with a larger group of older children, some playing the part of buns and others acting as customers choosing a bun to 'take away'.

FOUNDATION STAGE PROFILE LINKS
Calculating
• • • • • •
2 Recognises differences in quantity when comparing sets of objects.
• • • • • •
4 Relates addition to combining two groups.

GROUP SIZE
Four children.

TIMING
Ten to 15 minutes.

ASSESSMENT
Does the child recognise the difference between two unequal groups of objects, for example, a field of three sheep and a field of six cows? (2)

Is the child able to calculate how many objects there are in two groups by combining them and counting them, for example, the number of toy sheep and cows altogether? (4)

HOME LINKS
Encourage parents and carers to use appropriate language with their children, such as 'more' or 'less', when comparing groups of everyday objects, for example, when serving meals.

COWS AND SHEEP

Learning objective
To use language such as 'more' or 'less' to compare two numbers.

What you need
Cows and sheep from a small-world farm (different quantities, but no more than ten of each); miniature farm fencing.

What to do
Tip the cows and sheep on to the floor and invite the children to sort them into two separate piles. Show the children the plastic fences and explain that the farmer wants to keep the cows and sheep separate from each other. Ask the children for suggestions about how this can be done using the fences in front of them.

Try out the children's suggestions and encourage them to create two separate fields. Put the sheep in one field and the cows in the other. Ask the children questions such as, 'Which field has the most animals?' and 'Are there more sheep or more cows?'. Count the sheep and then the cows to find out if the children's guesses were correct. Can the children tell which field has the smallest number of animals without counting again?

Support
With younger children, work with up to five of each animal and make the contrasts greater, for example, two cows and five sheep. Take the animals out of the field and stand them alongside one another so that differences in quantity are more obvious.

Extension
Challenge older children to solve more complex problems. Invite them to sort the same type of animal by size or colour into separate enclosures and then try to discover which enclosure has the most and which has the least in it. Finally, ask the children to combine the two and see how many they have altogether.

FOUNDATION STAGE PROFILE LINKS

Calculating

• • • • • •

3 Finds one more or one less from a group of up to 5 objects.

• • • • • •

8 Finds one more or one less than a number from 1 to 10.

GROUP SIZE

Four children.

TIMING

20 minutes.

ASSESSMENT
Is the child able to work out what is one more or one less than a number from 1 to 5 (3), and up to 10 (8), for example, when deciding how many biscuits will be left on a plate if a child takes one?

TIME FOR A SNACK

Learning objective
To find one more or one less than a number from 1 to 10.

What you need
Children's plates and cups; snack food such as cheese, oranges and apples; bowls.

Preparation
Prepare a session snack with a small group of children beforehand, for example, peel and cut fruit into small portions and create cheese cubes. Refrigerate the food until snack time.

What to do
Explain that you have already prepared the snack, but that you would like your helpers to share it out equally. Consider any allergies, dietary requirements and special needs that those present might have, and provide alternatives if necessary.

Decide together how many to prepare for by counting the number of children on the register. Invite the helpers to set a place for every child by putting chairs around tables. Encourage them to solve any problems that they encounter, for example, what to do if there are too many, or not enough, chairs.

When the other children are seated, invite the helpers to give out the food and drink, taking care to ensure that each child is given the same amount. Encourage the helpers to ask you for what they need, for example, 'One more piece of apple'.

Support
Invite younger children to set up a dolls' tea party for three dolls. Organise resources to ensure that they will need to ask for 'one more' item, for example, by putting out only two plates to start with.

Extension
Provide more opportunities for older children to work out how many there will be if one object is taken away, or if one object is added, for example, shortening a toy train with four trucks by taking one away so that there are three trucks.

HOME LINKS

Encourage parents and carers to play games with their children involving adding one more object or taking one away, for example, when building towers of bricks.

FOUNDATION STAGE PROFILE LINKS
Calculating

• • • • • •

5 Relates subtraction to taking away.

• • • • • •

7 Finds one more or one less than a number from 1 to 10.

GROUP SIZE
Up to six children.

TIMING
20 minutes.

ASSESSMENT
Can the child say how many objects are left when some are taken away, for example, when he or she counts instruments on a table, one is hidden behind a screen, and then he or she counts those that are left?

HOME LINKS
Suggest that parents and carers play 'Kim's game' with their children by putting a number of everyday objects on a tray and covering them with a cloth. The adult then takes one object from under the cloth and asks the child to guess what has gone. Encourage them to use mathematical vocabulary such as 'Take one away' and 'How many are left?'.

WHAT'S MISSING?

Learning objective
To begin to relate addition to combining two groups of objects and subtraction to 'taking away'.

What you need
Ten different musical instruments; low table; screen.

What to do
Arrange the instruments on a low table in front of the screen and ask the children to sit in front of it. Look at the instruments together, name them and listen to the sound that each one makes.

Invite the children to close their eyes while you take one instrument away and hide it behind the screen. Ask them to open their eyes and guess which object has gone. If they find this difficult, give them a sound clue by playing the instrument behind the screen. Continue to remove instruments, one by one, talking about 'taking one away from the table' as you do so.

When all the instruments are behind the screen, reverse the activity until the table is full again, using the appropriate vocabulary, such as 'I'm going to add one more instrument to the table'.

Count the items on the table before and after one is taken away, or before and after one has been put back, using the appropriate vocabulary, for example, 'Open your eyes again, we have one less (or one more) now. Let's see how many we have on the table'.

Support
With younger children, start with fewer instruments on the table so that it is easier to identify which one has been taken away each time.

Extension
Encourage older children to organise the game themselves, taking turns to take an instrument away and put it behind the screen.

MATCHING TOWERS

Learning objective
To use developing mathematical ideas and methods to solve practical problems.

What you need
Twenty wooden or plastic cubes.

What to do
Invite the children to work in pairs and give each pair ten cubes. Suggest that they build a tower with the cubes.

Look at the two towers together. Are they the same height? If not, ask the children if they can make them the same by adding cubes to the shorter tower or taking cubes away from the taller tower. Use appropriate vocabulary as the children are working, such as, 'Maisy and Saheed had three bricks in their short tower and added two more to make it the same as Will and Sally's tall tower. Three and two make five. Has the tall tower got five bricks?'. Once the towers are the same, check again by counting the number of cubes in each one.

Support
Work with two younger children with five cubes each. Ask them to make a tower with the cubes and then see if they are the same height. What happens if one child takes away a cube? Are the towers the same height now? How can they make them the same again?

Extension
Challenge older children with problems using cubes of two different colours. Give them ten blue and ten yellow cubes each and ask them to try to build towers ten cubes high from different colour combinations, for example, six blue and four yellow or nine yellow and one blue. Invite them to record their results on squared paper with blue and yellow crayons.

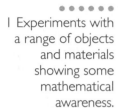

ROLLING OR SLIDING?

Learning objective

To use developing mathematical ideas and methods to solve practical problems.

What you need

Selection of cubes such as plastic play cubes, large dice and recycled boxes; selection of spheres such as balls of different sizes and marbles; plank of wood; wooden crates; large drawstring bag or pillowcase.

Preparation

Put the spheres and cubes into the large bag. Balance the plank on the crates to form a ramp with a steep-enough gradient for a cardboard box to slide down.

What to do

Show the children the ramp. Explain to them that you have filled a bag with lots of different things and that you would like them to help you to decide which things will roll and which things will slide down the ramp. Invite the children to take turns to pull something out of the bag and see what happens when they put the object at the top of the ramp. Does it roll or slide down?

Suggest that you sort the objects into two types: things that 'roll' and things that 'slide'. Talk about other things that the children are familiar with, such as to sort cutlery and toy animals.

Explain that the two different kinds of objects are 'cubes' and 'spheres'. Talk about the properties of a cube. Why does it slide rather than roll? Compare it to a sphere. Does this have edges and corners?

ASSESSMENT

Does the child demonstrate an interest in shape and space, for example, as he or she tries to roll cubes and spheres down a ramp? (1)

Is the child able to recognise similarities and differences in objects and sort them accordingly? Can he or she give reasons for his or her actions, for example, when sorting spheres and cubes into two groups according to whether they will roll or not? (2)

Support

Invite younger children to sort balls of two different colours or sizes into separate containers.

Extension

Invite older children to create patterns by threading beads of different shapes, sizes or colours alternately along a lace.

FOUNDATION STAGE PROFILE LINKS

Shape, space and measures

● ● ● ● ● ●

3 Describes shapes in simple models, pictures and patterns.

● ● ● ● ● ●

6 Uses language such as 'circle' or 'bigger' to describe the shape and size of solids and flat shapes.

● ● ● ● ● ●

9 Uses mathematical language to describe solid (3-D) objects and flat (2-D) shapes.

GROUP SIZE
Four children.

TIMING
20 minutes.

ASSESSMENT

Does the child describe shapes in everyday language, for example, saying that an object is 'round and round'? (3)

Does the child use appropriate language to describe the shape and size of solids and flat shapes, for example, describing the sides of a cube as 'flat' or 'straight' with corners? (6)

Can the child name common 2-D shapes such as a circle, triangle and square, and 3-D objects such as a sphere, cylinder and cube? (9)

HOME LINKS
Encourage parents and carers to point out and name common 2-D and 3-D shapes and to talk about the properties of these shapes with their children.

GUESS WHICH ONE

Learning objective
To use language such as 'circle' or 'bigger' to describe the shape and size of solids and flat shapes.

What you need
Two boxes, one with a lid; pairs of objects of regular shapes such as a sphere (ball), cylinder (cardboard tube), cube (plastic play cube) and cuboid (box from toothpaste tube).

Preparation
Cut a round hole in the lid of one of the boxes, large enough for the objects to be posted through. Put one of each of the shapes into the box and place matching shaped objects into the box without a lid.

What to do
Invite the children to take turns to put a hand through the hole in the box lid and choose a shape to feel and describe. Invite the others to choose a matching shape from the open box. Check their choice by pulling the hidden shape through the hole.

When all the shapes have been matched, help the children to name them.

Compare two matching shapes. Ask the children which is the biggest, or whether they are both the same size. Talk about the differences in the shapes.

Support
With younger children, concentrate on comparing the sizes of the objects, rather than naming them. Use the words 'biggest', 'bigger', 'smallest' and 'smaller'.

Extension
Invite older children to search through recycled materials, such as cartons and tubes, to find further examples of three-dimensional shapes.

FOUNDATION STAGE PROFILE LINKS
Shape, space and measures

• • • • • •

4 Talks about, recognises and re-creates simple patterns.

GROUP SIZE
Four children.

TIMING
Ten to 15 minutes to create the rollers; 15 minutes to make patterns with them.

ASSESSMENT
Is the child able to recognise and describe a simple pattern, for example, on fabric prints or when printing a repeat pattern with a roller?

HOME LINKS
Encourage parents and carers to draw their children's attention to patterns in the environment, for example, the arrangement of bricks in a wall or colours in a stained-glass window.

ROLLING PATTERNS

Learning objective
To talk about, recognise and re-create simple patterns.

What you need
Clean, empty plastic lemonade bottles; string; PVA glue; shallow tray; thick paint; paper.

What to do
Invite each child to create a paint roller by covering a plastic bottle with a thick layer of PVA glue and attaching string to it. Encourage the children to experiment with sticking the string to the bottle in different ways, for example, by winding a length of string in a spiral around the bottle starting at one end and pressing the string down until it reaches the other end, by making circles with separate lengths of string around the bottle, or by attaching separate long strips from one end to the other. Allow the string to dry thoroughly.

Return to the activity when the rollers are dry and pour some paint into a shallow tray. Supply the children with some paper and invite them to choose a paint roller each. Move the rollers backwards and forwards in the paint until the string is well coated. Put the roller on the paper and roll it in one direction. Encourage the children to talk about, and compare, the patterns that they have created. Show them how to re-create a mirror image of the pattern by pressing another piece of paper on top of the pattern and peeling it off to reveal a print.

Extend the activity by introducing a different paint colour in a separate tray. Observe the patterns created by printing with another colour over the first pattern.

Support
Make the rollers for younger children and encourage them to discover the different patterns that they can create by pushing them across a flattened piece of play dough.

Extension
Encourage older children to experiment further with pattern-making by gluing small circles of sponge between the string on their rollers, or in rows on a separate bottle.

FOUNDATION STAGE PROFILE LINKS

Shape, space and measures

• • • • • •

5 Uses everyday words to describe position.

GROUP SIZE
Four children.

TIMING
20 minutes.

ASSESSMENT

Can the child understand, and sometimes use, everyday language to describe position, for example, when describing the movements of a doll over an obstacle course, or when following an instruction to find an object?

UP AND UNDER

Learning objective
To use everyday words to describe position.

What you need
Short planks; cardboard boxes; small hoops; large apparatus, such as a climbing frame, barrel, tunnel and hoops; dolls and teddies.

Preparation
Set up an obstacle course with the selection of large apparatus. Let the children play on the course before the planned activity, having fun negotiating it.

What to do
Ask the children to recall what they did on the obstacle course that they negotiated before the activity. Use positional language as you remind them about how they went 'through' the tunnel, 'down' the slide and 'under' the climbing frame.

Suggest to the children that they make a miniature obstacle course for dolls and teddies to negotiate, using a selection of boxes, planks and hoops. Encourage the children to try out different ideas as they build the course, for example, creating a slide from a box and a plank, a tunnel from an open box and a balance beam from a plank between two boxes.

Invite each child to choose a doll or teddy to 'help' to move across the obstacle course. Emphasise positional language as the children move the toys, for example, 'I am watching your teddy crawling *under* the chair and *through* the tunnel. He is managing very well', 'Your doll is walking very carefully *along* the top of the bench' and 'Can your teddy manage to go *down* the slide?'.

Support
Play games with younger children using a small table, a chair and a doll. Ask them to put the doll in the position that you indicate, for example, 'under the chair' or 'on the table'.

Extension
With older children, extend positional language to include, for example, 'between', 'beside', 'behind', 'forwards' and 'backwards', and encourage them to use these words as they describe a physical journey across large apparatus.

HOME LINKS
Suggest to parents and carers that they use positional language when giving their children instructions to find a hidden object, for example, 'Look behind the chair'.

FOUNDATION STAGE PROFILE LINKS

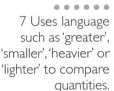

Shape, space and measures

• • • • • •

7 Uses language such as 'greater', 'smaller', 'heavier' or 'lighter' to compare quantities.

GROUP SIZE
Four children.

TIMING
20 minutes.

ASSESSMENT
Does the child understand, and sometimes use, appropriate language to compare quantities, for example, remarking that one of the buckets on a bucket balance is 'heavier' than the other when more sand is added?

SAND LIFTERS

Learning objective
To use language such as 'greater', 'smaller', 'heavier' or 'lighter' to compare quantities.

What you need
Sand tray; sand; bucket balance; sand scoops.

What to do
Allow time for the children to play freely with the bucket balance in the sand area at the start of the activity. Encourage them to talk about their observations by asking them appropriate questions, such as, 'What is happening to this bucket?' and 'Why has this bucket moved down?'.

Introduce the word 'balance' and demonstrate the meaning, by emptying the two buckets so that they are level. Ask a child to put a scoop of sand into one bucket and describe to the others what has happened. Can they say which they think is the heaviest bucket?

Take the two buckets off the balance and let the children lift them up to test their decision. Was their choice correct? Which is the lightest? Can they say why?

Return the buckets to the balance and ask another child to put a scoop of sand into the empty bucket. Do the buckets balance? If necessary, add sand slowly until they do. Do the children know how to make one side heavier or lighter than the other by adding or removing sand?

Introduce the words 'more' and 'less', and 'greater' and 'smaller' to compare the quantities of sand in each bucket.

Support
Encourage younger children to play freely with scoops and buckets in the sand and talk about putting 'more' sand in the buckets to fill them up. Talk about the buckets being 'too heavy' to lift up and ask the children to take some of the sand back out again.

Extension
Extend play beyond the sand tray with older children by asking them to weigh and balance small objects, such as plastic bears, in a bucket balance.

HOME LINKS

Encourage parents and carers to model appropriate language, for example, when asking their children to weigh and measure ingredients for a recipe.

IT'S A WRAP

Learning objective
To use developing mathematical ideas and methods to solve practical problems.

What you need
Role-play post office: three screens; two child-size tables; post-box; sack; postperson's hat; tabard; paper; envelopes; pencils; telephone; till; items of unsolicited mail; rubber stamp; ink pad; used stamps; scales. Parcels: small boxes of varying sizes; brown paper; parcel tape; scissors; pens; glue sticks.

Preparation
Set up a role-play post office using resources such as those listed above. Put the resources for the post-office counter on one table and the letter-writing resources on the other. Stand the post-box alongside.

What to do
Show the children the post office that you have set up and explain that you did not have enough time to create some parcels for the children to pretend to post.

Look at the parcel-wrapping resources together and invite each child to choose a box to wrap up. What shape is it? Is it big or small? Talk about how much paper will be needed to cover the box and help the child to cut this if necessary. Decide where to put the box on the piece of brown paper, and how to fold the paper over it. How will the child secure the paper?

Encourage the children to try out their ideas and praise them for their efforts, even if it takes several attempts to succeed. As you talk to the children, try to incorporate vocabulary related to shape, size, position and quantity.

Help each child to write the name of the recipient on the outside of the parcel, and invite them to take it to the post office to be weighed and stamped.

Support
Pre-cut the brown paper for younger children and hold the parcel and tape steady for them as they fold and stick the parcel.

Extension
Leave the parcel-making resources near to the post-office area so that older children can incorporate this activity into their role-play.

CHAPTER 4

Knowledge and understanding of the world

Help the children to find out about the world around them with these activities, which offer opportunities to assess their progress as they play.

FOUNDATION STAGE PROFILE LINKS

1 Shows curiosity and interest by exploring surroundings.

• • • • • •

2 Observes, selects and manipulates objects and materials. Identifies simple features and significant personal events.

GROUP SIZE

Up to six children.

TIMING

Ten to 15 minutes.

ASSESSMENT

Does the child demonstrate curiosity and interest by exploring surroundings, for example, when hunting for minibeasts? (1)

Does the child observe, select and manipulate objects and materials, and describe simple features of objects and events, for example, when choosing a magnifying glass to observe the segments of a worm? Does the child sometimes link experiences, observations and events, for example, remembering past experiences of similar creatures? (2)

HOME LINKS

Suggest to parents and carers that they take their children on a 'minibeast hunt' in their gardens or nearby parks.

MINIATURE WORLDS

Learning objective

To find out about, and identify, some features of living things, objects and events they observe.

What you need

Bug viewers; magnifying glasses; paper; pencils; crayons; plastic containers; books about minibeasts.

Preparation

Choose an appropriate area where the children will be able to find small creatures.

What to do

Take the children outdoors and suggest that they look under stones or logs to search for small creatures. Explain how to handle the creatures gently and put them into plastic containers with the tops securely covered.

Take the creatures indoors and invite the children to observe them with magnifying glasses and bug viewers. Use books to identify the creatures. Discuss their different features and make observational drawings.

Return the creatures to their habitat afterwards.

Support

Take young children to observe and name creatures without moving them from their habitat. Talk about features such as tiny feelers. Be sensitive to those who might be afraid, and give lots of reassurance.

Extension

Ask older children to record the creatures in a given area by marking them on a tick chart.

FOUNDATION STAGE PROFILE LINKS

3 Constructs in a purposeful way, using simple tools and techniques.

• • • • • •

8 Builds and constructs with a wide range of objects, selecting appropriate resources, tools and techniques and adapting her/his work where necessary.

• • • • • •

9 Communicates simple planning for investigations and constructions and makes simple records and evaluations of her/his work.

GROUP SIZE
Four children.

TIMING
20 minutes.

ASSESSMENT
Does the child construct purposefully, using appropriate tools and techniques, for example, when designing an animal cage? (3)

Does the child make use of the resources and tools available, and appropriate techniques, adapting his or her work where necessary, for example, deciding to use a smaller box for a mouse cage? (8)

Is the child able to explain how he or she planned a construction, such as a cage, and make simple records and evaluations of the work? (9)

HOME LINKS

Invite carers to take their children to observe a range of cages in a pet shop.

THE PET SHOP

Learning objective
To build and construct with a wide range of objects, selecting appropriate resources, and adapting their work where necessary.

What you need
Role-play pet shop: screens; small tables; till; telephone; toy money; paper; pencils; dog leads; food bowls; toys. Cages: recycled boxes and cartons; glue; tape; scissors; string; art straws; straw or fabric pieces for bedding; soft toys to represent pets.

Preparation
Set up a role-play pet shop using the resources suggested above.

What to do
Show the children the pet shop and explain that you would like them to create cages for the pets.

Invite each child to choose a 'pet' and work freely with the resources to try out their cage-building ideas. Make suggestions constructively, for example, using art straws to create the cage bars.

Put each 'pet' in a cage, along with some bedding, and arrange the cages in the pet shop.

Support
Simplify the activity for younger children, for example, asking them to help you to glue strips of paper across the fronts of cages.

Extension
Challenge older children to choose the most appropriate tools and materials for the cage-making task, and encourage them to give reasons for their choices.

FOUNDATION STAGE PROFILE LINKS

4 Investigates places, objects, materials and living things, by using all the senses as appropriate. Identifies some features and talks about those features s/he likes and dislikes.

· · · · · ·

9 Identifies and names key features and properties, sometimes linking different experiences, observations and events.

GROUP SIZE

Up to six children; one adult for every two children.

TIMING

20 minutes for the walk; ten minutes for later discussion.

ASSESSMENT

Is the child able to identify some of the features observed when investigating places, objects, materials and living things? Does he or she talk about his or her likes and dislikes? (4)

Does the child identify and name key features and properties, such as buildings with different functions, and sometimes link experiences, observations and events, for example, recalling a past experience of a festival after observing a community carnival? (9)

HOME LINKS

Encourage parents and carers to take their children to local places of interest, such as zoos, parks and shops.

A LOCAL WALK

Learning objective

To observe, find out about and identify features in the place they live and the natural world.

What you need

A camera; pencils; paper; paints; sugar paper.

What to do

Take the children for a walk in the immediate locality, for example, to a park or along the street. Stop and talk about the different features of the environment, such as roads, railways, shops, places of worship, houses, trees and rivers. Encourage the children to discuss what they like and dislike about what they see, for example, flowers in the park or litter in the street.

Invite the children to take turns to take photographs of these features. As you return to your setting, continue to discuss the outing and recall previous outings.

Have the film developed and show the photographs to the children, encouraging them to recall their outing as you look at them together. Invite them to draw and paint pictures of the things that they liked and disliked about what they observed. Create a book made from sugar paper and attach the children's work and the photographs inside it, or make a wall display together.

Support

Take a shorter walk with younger children and concentrate on naming the features rather than discussing likes and dislikes.

Extension

Take photographs and go on a walk of discovery with older children to search for the features depicted. Draw a plan of the route taken.

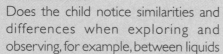
CHANGING COLOURS

Learning objectives
To look closely at similarities, differences, patterns and change; to ask questions about why things happen and how things work.

What you need
A water tray; plastic spoons; small bowls; various food colourings; freezer.

Preparation
Half-fill small bowls with water and add a few drops of different food colouring to each one. Put the bowls in the freezer until required. Check for any allergies to food colouring.

What to do
Put some warm water in the water tray and invite the children to put their hands in. Is it hot, cold or warm? Tip a bowl-shaped block of ice into the tray and ask the children to stir it around with spoons. Explain that they should not touch ice straight from the freezer as it may hurt their fingers.

Ask the children to observe what happens to the colour of the water. Why do they think it is changing? Introduce the words 'melt', 'frozen', 'solid' and 'liquid'. Do the children notice anything about the temperature of the water? Is it still warm?

Add a different coloured ice block. What happens when this begins to melt? Discuss the changing colour of the water, for example, does blue and red ice melt to form purple water?

Invite the children to choose the ice colours to add and try to predict what will happen to the colour of the water.

Support
Add drops of colouring directly to the water with young children as handling ice can burn their fingers.

Extension
Invite older children to fill jelly moulds with coloured water, then freeze them to create unusual ice shapes to float in the water.

FOUNDATION STAGE PROFILE LINKS

6 Finds out about past and present events in own life, and in those of family members and other people s/he knows. Begins to know about own culture and beliefs and those of other people.

• • • • • •

9 Begins to explore what it means to belong to a variety of groups and communities.

GROUP SIZE

Six children to prepare; whole group for visit.

TIMING

20 minutes to prepare; 45 minutes for visit.

ASSESSMENT

Does the child show interest in past and present events, for example, by listening to a grandparent talking about toys that he or she played with as a child? (6)

Does the child demonstrate a growing awareness of his or her own culture and beliefs and those of other people, for example, when talking about a family naming ceremony? (9)

HOME LINKS

Encourage elderly family members to bring in photographs and mementoes of their past to show to the children.

GRANDPARENTS' DAY

Learning objectives

To find out about past and present events in their own lives, and in those of their families and other people they know; to begin to know about their own cultures and beliefs and those of other people.

What you need

Fruit juice; snack, such as fruit pieces or biscuits; plates; cups; doilies; adult chairs.

Preparation

Send out invitations to grandparents and elderly friends, inviting them to a special morning to meet the children.

What to do

Talk to the children about their grandparents and elderly friends, and suggest that they invite them to visit and join some activities.

Ask a group of 'helpers' to prepare seating and a snack and drink before the visitors arrive. Encourage them to present the snack attractively, for example, by putting doilies on plates. Arrange adult seating in different play areas.

When the visitors arrive, suggest that they join the children at play and talk to them about their own childhood memories. Invite the helpers to serve the drink and snack that they have prepared.

Support

Ask a familiar adult to stay with younger children who do not have a special visitor of their own.

Extension

Encourage older children to discover more about their own past, for example, by looking at baby photographs of themselves.

GROUP SIZE
Four children.

TIMING
20 minutes.

ASSESSMENT
Is the child aware of some uses of technology, such as a computer, floor robot or tape recorder? Is he or she able to operate simple controls, for example, to record and play back sounds on a tape recorder?

SOUNDS INTERESTING!

Learning objective
To find out about and identify the uses of everyday technology and use information and communication technology and programmable toys to support their learning.

What you need
A battery-operated tape recorder; blank tapes; microphone; sound-effect 'Lotto' game.

What to do
Play the 'Lotto' game with the children. Then demonstrate how to operate the buttons on the tape recorder such as 'stop', 'start', 'pause', 'fast forward' and 'rewind', and how to increase and decrease the volume. Show the children the batteries in their compartment, and explain how to insert a tape and eject it. Play the 'Lotto' game again, choosing different children to press the relevant buttons, under your instruction.

Talk about other items of equipment that the children are familiar with that operate with buttons and switches. Do they have batteries, or do they plug into an electric socket? Discuss the uses, and the dangers, of electricity.

Show the children the microphone and explain its function. Invite a child to sing and demonstrate how to record this and play it back again. Encourage the children to take turns to sing while another child makes a recording under your supervision.

Explain that you are going to leave the tape recorder, microphone and recorded and blank tapes in a quiet corner for the children to operate themselves. Invite them to make recordings and to listen to pre-recorded tapes.

Support
Show younger children how to operate the 'stop' and 'start' buttons, and to insert and remove tapes, so that they can listen to pre-recorded stories and music.

Extension
Encourage older children to take the tape recorder outdoors under adult supervision and to record the sounds that they hear. Suggest that they play these back to their friends to see if they can identify them.

HOME LINKS
Encourage parents and carers to talk to their children about the safe use of technology in the home, and to invite them to operate buttons and switches, for example, on a torch or camera.

CHAPTER 5

Assess the children's physical skills during these activities, planned to develop a range of small- and large-motor skills.

Physical development

FOUNDATION STAGE PROFILE LINKS
I Moves spontaneously, showing some control and co-ordination.

GROUP SIZE
Up to ten children.

TIMING
20 minutes.

ASSESSMENT
Does the child respond through appropriate movement, for example, to different kinds of music and rhythm? Does he or she generally create intended body movements, for example, moving smoothly to represent the movement of liquid, and standing still after hearing a given signal?

HOME LINKS
Encourage parents and carers to dance with their children to different kinds of music, and to play games such as 'Musical bumps' to develop bodily control.

FROZEN TO THE SPOT

Learning objectives
To move with control and co-ordination; to move with confidence, imagination and in safety.

What you need
A water tray; triangle; metal beater; drum; tape recorder; recorded music to represent flowing water, such as *Pavane* by Fauré; ice cubes; jug.

Preparation
Freeze some ice cubes.

What to do
Invite the children to watch as you slowly pour water from a height into a water tray. Discuss the noise and movement of the water travelling from jug to tray. Introduce the word 'liquid' and ask the children to name other liquids.

Fill the jug with ice cubes and tip these from the same height. Make comparisons between the sound and movement of water and ice. Does the ice flow in the same way? Introduce the word 'solid'. What happens if the ice is left in a warm place? Introduce the word 'melt'.

Invite the children to pretend to be liquid, flowing freely to the music that you are going to play. Encourage them to move their bodies gently and smoothly.

Stop the music and ask the children to listen to the sound of the triangle. Explain that when they hear this 'icy' sound, they should freeze, just like a big ice cube. Now beat a drum with the palm of your hand and explain that this 'warm' sound means that the ice cubes are melting.

Invite the children to move to the music once again, freezing to the sound of the triangle and melting to the beat of the drum.

Support
Develop younger children's bodily control by inviting them to dance spontaneously to some lively music until it stops, and then stand still as quickly as they can.

Extension
Plan this activity to follow 'Changing colours' (page 66) so that older children can experience how coloured ice melts at first hand.

FOUNDATION STAGE PROFILE LINKS

2 Moves with confidence in a variety of ways, showing some awareness of space.

• • • • • •

4 Moves with confidence, imagination and in safety. Travels around, under, over and through balancing and climbing equipment. Shows awareness of space, of self and others.

• • • • • •

9 Repeats, links and adapts simple movements, sometimes commenting on her/his work. Demonstrates co-ordination and control in large and small movements, and using a range of tools and equipment.

GROUP SIZE
Four children.

TIMING
Ten to 15 minutes.

HOME LINKS
Encourage parents and carers to take their children to parks and soft play centres to experience a variety of climbing and balancing opportunities.

DOWN IN THE JUNGLE

Learning objectives
To move with confidence, imagination and in safety; to travel around, under, over and through balancing and climbing equipment.

What you need
A selection of large apparatus, such as a climbing frame, bench and barrel; safety mats.

Preparation
Set out the apparatus as a jungle, for example, with a climbing frame 'tree', a safety mat 'pool' and 'fallen log' benches.

What to do
Talk to the children about jungle life. Can they name some animals, birds and reptiles who live there?

Explain that you have created a 'pretend' jungle so that the children can be visiting explorers or jungle creatures. Allow time for them to play freely and encourage different movements by suggestion, for example, 'This space is perfect for a snake to slide under' or 'A crocodile might be hiding in this pool, better tiptoe around it!'.

Support
Ensure that the apparatus is at an appropriate height for younger children and support them if they lack confidence.

Extension
Encourage older children to try different ways of moving across apparatus, for example, sliding like a snake or swinging like a monkey.

ASSESSMENT
Does the child move confidently in a variety of ways, showing some awareness of space, for example, when sharing the same piece of apparatus with other children? (2)

Does the child move imaginatively and safely? Does he or she move across balancing and climbing equipment in different ways, for example, under, over, around and through it? (4)

Is the child able to repeat, link and modify movements, sometimes talking about her or his actions, for example, when deciding the most appropriate way to negotiate a piece of equipment? Does the child demonstrate increasing co-ordination and control in large and small movements, for example, combining several different ways of negotiating a role-play jungle? (9)

POTATO PICKERS

Learning objective
To use a range of small and large equipment.

What you need
Four buckets; sack; potatoes.

Preparation
Spread the potatoes in four regular rows across a large floor space.

What to do
Invite the children to sit at one side of the floor space and put the sack at the other. Explain that the floor is the farmer's field and that the children are going to help the farmer to pick the potato crop.

Supply the children with a bucket each and ask them to move along a row of potatoes, bending down to pick them up and put them into their buckets. At the end of the row, they should tip the potatoes into the sack and run back to where they started.

Support
Reduce the number of potatoes for younger children to pick up.

Extension
With older children, extend the activity into a team game. Arrange the potatoes in two rows of nine and divide six children into two teams. Invite team members to take turns to pick up three potatoes, put them in the bucket, tip them in the sack and return with the empty bucket for the next child to use.

ASSESSMENT

Is the child able to negotiate a space, changing speed and direction if necessary to avoid other children and obstacles, for example, when playing the potato-picking game? (3)

Does the child show increasing control when using small and large equipment, and demonstrate a growing range of basic skills, for example, picking up potatoes and putting them in a bucket? (6)

Does the child repeat, link and alter movements, sometimes talking about actions? Does he or she demonstrate co-ordination and control in large and small movements and when using different tools and equipment, for example, changing hands to tip potatoes from a bucket into a sack because it is more effective? (9)

FOUNDATION STAGE PROFILE LINKS

5 Demonstrates fine motor control and co-ordination.

● ● ● ● ● ●

7 Handles tools, objects, construction and malleable materials safely and with basic control.

GROUP SIZE
Four children.

TIMING
20 minutes.

WOOD SCULPTURES

Learning objective
To handle tools, objects, construction and malleable materials safely and with increasing control.

What you need
Offcuts of soft wood; sandpaper; PVA glue; glue spreaders; small natural items such as twigs, conkers, ash keys and acorns.

Preparation
Ensure that there are no rough or sharp edges on the wood. Create four sanding blocks by attaching sandpaper to wood offcuts with glue.

What to do
Invite the children to pass around the pieces of wood and to talk about how they feel, look and smell. Demonstrate how sandpaper or a sanding block can be used to smooth wood by rubbing it against the surface. Ask the children to choose a piece of wood to sand.

Show them the selection of natural items. See how many they can name and discuss the shape, size, smell, texture and appearance of each one. Invite the children to choose different items to stick to the surface of their wood to create unusual sculptures and models.

Support
Give younger children ready-sanded wood blocks and invite them to attach their choice of natural items.

Extension
Introduce tools such as a vice, file and hand drill to older children so that they can create sculptures by shaping their wood and forming holes in the surface.

ASSESSMENT
Does the child demonstrate fine motor control and co-ordination when handling small objects, for example, when he or she is gluing twigs and conkers to pieces of wood? (5)

Does the child handle tools, objects, construction and malleable materials safely and with basic control, for example, when using sandpaper or sand blocks to smooth wood? (7)

HOME LINKS
Encourage carers to demonstrate to their children how to use simple tools, such as scissors, hand whisks and pastry cutters.

FOUNDATION STAGE PROFILE LINKS
8 Recognises the importance of keeping healthy and those things which contribute to this.

GROUP SIZE
Four children.

TIMING
20 minutes.

ASSESSMENT
Does the child indicate a growing awareness of factors that contribute to a healthy lifestyle, for example, a good balanced diet?

VARIETY SNACKS

Learning objective
To recognise the importance of keeping healthy and those things which contribute to this.

What you need
Pictures in magazines of a wide variety of healthy snacks, for example, fruit, vegetables, pasta, rice, breads, potatoes and dairy foods; card; glue stick; felt-tipped pen; large sheet of card.

Preparation
Look through magazines to find pictures of foods suitable for healthy snacks. Cut these out and mount them on card.

What to do
Explain to the children that you would like them to help you to plan out the selection of snacks for the following week. Look through the pictures and talk about the important contribution that a balanced diet makes towards a healthy lifestyle.

Invite the children to choose pictures of things that they would like to include on their menu. Spread them out and decide whether there is a good variety of different foods amongst the choices, for example, some fruit, vegetables, bread, crackers, yoghurt and cheese.

Explain that the children will be attending for five days the next week and so you will need to decide on five different snacks. Select five of the chosen picture cards, then arrange these in order, for example, alternating fresh fruit with a starchy snack such as crackers.

Attach the pictures to a large sheet of card in the appropriate order and write the names of the days above them. Include a caption, such as 'The snacks for this week were chosen by...', and add the children's names.

Plan alternative snacks for children who have specific dietary requirements or food allergies.

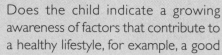

Support
Encourage younger children to name the foods in the pictures and plan sessions to introduce them gradually to new taste sensations.

Extension
Involve older children in purchasing items for their chosen snacks and helping to prepare them.

HOME LINKS
Emphasise to parents and carers the importance of developing their children's awareness of the things that contribute to a healthy lifestyle, such as a balanced diet, regular sleep and exercise, and good personal hygiene.

FOUNDATION STAGE PROFILE LINKS

8 Recognises the changes that happen to her/his body when s/he is active.

GROUP SIZE

Up to 12 children.

TIMING

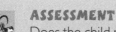

Ten to 15 minutes.

ASSESSMENT

Does the child notice the changes that happen to his or her body when he or she is active, for example, before and after a period of vigorous exercise?

WARM-UP TIME

Learning objective

To recognise the changes that happen to their bodies when they are active.

What you need

A clear space, either indoors or outdoors.

What to do

Take the children outdoors if possible, or clear a large floor space indoors. Begin the activity with some warming-up exercises. Invite the children to stretch their arms up high above their heads, and then slowly lower them again. Follow this by asking them to shake one foot and then the other.

Talk about how these exercises help their bodies to warm up before they start to run and jump around. Can they feel their muscles stretching? Do they feel any warmer?

Ask the children to run, jump, hop or skip freely until they hear a given signal, such as a clap, and then to stand still. How do they feel after this activity? Talk about feeling hot and 'out of breath'. Show the children the position of their hearts and lungs and see if they can feel their chests rising and their hearts beating quickly.

Invite the children to unwind slowly with some more stretching exercises. Ask them what has happened to their breathing and heart rate. Are they aware of any changes? Emphasise the importance of warming up and cooling down before vigorous exercise, and stress how regular exercise will help to keep their bodies strong and healthy.

Support

Talk in familiar language to younger children about how they feel after exercise, for example, tired and needing a rest, to raise their awareness of body changes.

Extension

Show older children how to feel their pulses with their fingers and listen to their heartbeats with a stethoscope. Encourage them to note changes before and after exercise.

HOME LINKS

Encourage parents and carers to take their children to parks and open spaces where they can enjoy moving freely.

CHAPTER 6

Encourage the children to explore a range of creative techniques to provide assessment opportunities across the whole Area of Learning.

Creative development

GARDEN ART

Learning objective
To explore colour, texture, shape, form and space in two or three dimensions.

What you need
Fresh flowers; vases; photographs of gardens; flower and bulb catalogues; crêpe paper; tissue; small collage materials such as buttons, sequins and glitter; various dried herbs and ground spices, such as mint, rosemary, basil, nutmeg, cinnamon and ginger; glue; scissors; thick paper.

Preparation
Invite parents and carers to loan photographs of their gardens with flowers in bloom and to supply fresh flowers. Display the flowers in vases. Check for any allergies to herbs and spices.

What to do
Show the children the flowers and talk about them. What colour are they? Do they have different smells? Pass around a flower and ask the children to describe what it feels like. Discuss the smells that they like or dislike. Look at the photographs and flower catalogues. Can the children find pictures of similar flowers? How many can they name?

Show the children the collage materials and paper and suggest that they create pictures of flowers using these materials. Encourage them to consider the colours and shapes of their flowers. When the pictures are finished ask the children to smell them. Do they have a perfume? Suggest creating a smell by adding something. Pass around the herbs and spices and invite the children to choose smells that they like. Show them how to spread glue on a flower and sprinkle a herb or spice on to it. Do they like the unusual scented flowers that they have created?

Support
With younger children, limit the selection of herbs and spices so that they can make choices easily.

Extension
Encourage older children to produce three-dimensional models of flowers with art straw stalks and tissue petals.

WEATHER SOUNDS

Learning objective
To sings simple songs from memory, recognise repeated sounds and sound patterns and match movements to music.

What you need
A selection of musical instruments; everyday resources to create sound effects, such as pan lids and spoons.

What to do
Invite the children to sing traditional weather-related rhymes, such as 'I Hear Thunder' and 'Incy Wincy Spider' (both Traditional), as an introduction to a discussion about different weather conditions.

Talk about the sounds made by wind, rain and thunder. Suggest to the children that they try to re-create these sounds using musical instruments, voices or everyday objects.

Explore the selection of instruments and ask the children to try to create the sound of heavy rain, for example, with a rainmaker. Can they create a similar sound with everyday items, such as rice grains falling on a metal pan lid? Can they make their voices sound like rain?

Continue to explore ways to represent weather sounds, for example, howling wind or crashing thunder. Sing the rhymes again, this time with the children's added sound effects.

Support
Help younger children to make wind chimes by attaching metal objects such as spoons, small bells and keys to a wire coat-hanger. Hang the chimes outdoors or in an open window.

Extension
Encourage older children to make up stories about different weather conditions, and invite them to re-enact them with their own sound effects.

OUR FAVOURITE MEMORIES

Learning objective

To express and communicate their ideas, thoughts and feelings by using a widening range of materials and suitable tools.

What you need

Wide selection of paper, for example, kitchen paper, texture wallpaper and sugar paper; white, red, yellow and blue paint; paint-mixing trays; paintbrushes of varying size and thickness.

Preparation

Take photographs during an outing and display them at child height. Cut the paper into various sizes and shapes.

What to do

Look at the photographs and ask the children for their favourite memories of the occasion. Suggest that they create personal reminders of the outing by painting pictures.

Explore the different types of paper together. Would paper with a 'bumpy' surface be suitable to paint a picture of a walk in the woods? Would smooth paper be more appropriate to paint a picnic on a bright sunny day? Encourage the children to consider the most appropriate colour, size and shape of paper for their own paintings.

Supply each child with a shallow tray and encourage them to experiment with mixing new colours from primary colours, adding white to create different shades.

Display the pictures alongside the photographs as 'Memories of a wonderful day'.

Support

Supply younger children with fewer choices, for example, two different papers and three paint colours, so that they begin to make decisions for themselves. Be ready to supply additional colours if they ask for them.

Extension

Show older children how to use paint techniques to create different effects, for example, blowing paint across paper with a straw to represent rain running down a window. Encourage them to use colour to represent feelings as well as objects.

AHOY THERE!

Learning objective

To use their imagination in art and design, music, dance, imaginative and role-play and stories.

What you need

Pictures of pirates; large packaging cartons; strong tape; broom handle; string; garden cane; white sheeting; pirate costumes, for example, waistcoats, woollen hats, headscarves and eye patches; small box; plastic jewellery.

Preparation

Ask parents and carers to help in supplying costumes and resources.

What to do

Talk to the children about what they know about pirates and suggest that they pretend to be pirates themselves. Look at the pictures and discuss how the children will dress and behave as pirates. This is an opportunity to discuss why it might not be a good idea to have daggers and swords. Explain that the children will have just as much fun sailing their pirate ship to look for treasure.

Create a pirate ship by fastening together the large cartons with strong tape. Add a broom-handle mast, securely taped to one of the cartons. Tape a length of garden cane across the top of the mast and tie a square of white sheeting to it to form a sail. Then add a flag made from the same material.

Put the jewellery in a small box and ask the children to close their eyes while you hide it somewhere near by.

Invite the children to dress up and climb aboard their pirate ship to go sailing the seas. When they arrive at a desert island, suggest that they swim ashore to search for hidden treasure!

Support

Younger children might find this role-play frightening. As an alternative, create a boat and pretend to sail to a desert island for a picnic.

Extension

Encourage older children to make up stories about their adventures aboard the pirate ship.

ASSESSMENT
Does the child express and
communicate ideas, thoughts and
feelings in a variety of ways, for example,
when creating puppets to represent the characters
in a story?

IT'S IN THE BAG!

Learning objective
To express and communicate their ideas, thoughts and feelings by using a widening range of materials, suitable tools, designing and making.

What you need
Copies of favourite stories with at least four characters; hand puppets; strong paper bags; collage materials such as fabric scraps, buttons and wool; scissors; PVA glue.

Preparation
Spend time reading the children's favourite stories leading up to the activity. Introduce the children to hand puppets by leaving some in the story corner for them to play with.

What to do
Ask the children to choose their favourite story and read it to them. Play briefly with the hand puppets again and suggest that the children might like to make some of their own to re-enact the story.

Make a list of the characters in the story. How many are there? Choose which character each child would like to make. Discuss any special features that the characters have, such as a beard, fur or long golden hair. Can the children suggest how they might represent these features using the materials available?

Show the children how they can make a simple puppet face from a paper bag by gluing their chosen collage materials to the paper bags to represent main features such as eyes, ears, nose, mouth and hair. Operate the puppet by putting a hand inside the bag and wiggling it backwards and forwards.

Invite the children to re-enact the story using the puppets that they have created.

Support
Encourage younger children to explore the resources freely to make simple puppets rather than specific characters.

Extension
Encourage older children to make up stories and to create their own puppets for these. Suggest that they put on a performance for younger children to watch.

9 Expresses feelings and preferences in response to artwork and makes some comparisons and links between different pieces. Responds to own work and that of others when exploring and communicating ideas, feelings and preferences through art.

GROUP SIZE

Four children.

TIMING

Ten to 15 minutes.

 ASSESSMENT
Does the child express feelings and personal preferences in response to artwork, and is he or she able to make comparisons and links between them, for example, commenting on similarities and differences when observing a selection of flower or animal paintings? Is the child developing an understanding of how paintings and pictures can express ideas, thoughts and feelings, for example, by discussing the work of artists and other children and his or her own work?

HOME LINKS

Encourage parents and carers to take their children to look at different artworks, for example, in art galleries and art shops, to widen their experience of how art and design can be used to express ideas, thoughts and feelings.

FAMOUS ARTISTS

Learning objective
To use their imagination in art and design.

What you need
Prints of the work of famous artists such as Monet, Klimt and Van Gogh; paper; paint; items to create appropriate painting techniques, such as sponge circles to print, and card combs and paint rollers to create patterns.

What to do
Look at the prints by famous artists, for example, the poppy series by Monet or the designs in the works of Klimt, and ask the children to talk about them. Do they like or dislike what they see? How do they think the artists created the pictures?

Suggest to the children that they choose a favourite print and try to create their own version of a similar subject using simple techniques, for example, representing poppies in a field by washing the paper with green and yellow paint and spattering bright red splashes over it, or combing green paint across some paper and using a sponge to print red circles on top.

Display the children's pictures around their chosen print with an explanation about the techniques used.

Support
Concentrate on paintings of flowers with younger children and talk about the colours they can see. Supply them with brightly coloured paints to create their own flower pictures.

Extension
Encourage older children to explore patterns and designs in pictures, wallpapers and fabrics, and suggest that they create their own patterns using rolling and printing techniques.